MW00909718

GOD'S
CHURCH
IN A HOSTILE
WORLD

GOD'S CHURCH IN A HOSTILE WORLD

Joseph J. Battistone, Ph.D.

REVIEW AND HERALD® PUBLISHING ASSOCIATION
WASHINGTON, DC 20039-0555
HAGERSTOWN, MD 21740

The author assumes full responsibility for the accuracy of all facts and quotations as cited in this book.

This book was
Edited by Gerald Wheeler
Designed by Bill Kirstein
Cover photo by Comstock, Inc. / Tom Ives
and Meylan Thoresen (inset)

Unless otherwise noted,
Bible texts in this book are from the Revised Standard Version of the Bible,
copyrighted 1946, 1952 © 1971, 1973.

PRINTED IN U.S.A.

R&H Cataloging Service
Battistone, Joseph J   1939—
  God's church in a hostile world.

  1. Bible N.T. Revelation   I-XI — Commentaries.
  I. Title.   228

ISBN 0-8280-0528-1

Dedication

IN LOVING MEMORY OF MY FATHER

Peter L. Battistone, Sr.

Revelation 14:13

Acknowledgments

This book is a humble effort to provide supplementary reading to the Sabbath school lesson quarterly on the first half of the book of Revelation (chapters 1-11). In preparing the material, I have sought to point out the significant part the Old Testament has played in providing the language and imagery for John's message, and to emphasize the positive character of the book. For those who have "ears to hear," the book of Revelation may be seen as a great source of comfort, joy, and strength for troubled times.

For the most part, I have chosen to follow the Revised Standard Version of the Bible, because it has been the text traditionally used in Bible classes of English-speaking Seventh-day Adventist colleges. In addition, I have frequently consulted the Seventh-day Adventist Bible Commentary Series, The Daily Study Bible Series, by William Barclay, the work by Robert H. Mounce in *The International Commentary on the New Testament*, and *The Letters to the Seven Churches*, by William M. Ramsay.

I wish to express appreciation to Mrs. Penny Estes Wheeler for her helpful suggestions as to style and substance, but at the same time, I claim full responsibility for the book's weaknesses and imperfections.

In conclusion, I offer my sincere gratitude to my wife, Adrienne, and to my children, Michael and Rochelle, for their positive support to me and their patient understanding of the time pressures on me during the preparation of this manuscript.

It is my supreme desire that the readers will find this book to be a guide to understanding the book of Revelation as a pertinent and practical message for our troubled times.

Joseph J. Battistone
Hendersonville, North Carolina

Contents

Revelation
and Response

(Based on Revelation 1:1-8)

"So shall my word be that goes forth from my mouth; it shall not return to me empty" *(Isa. 55:11).*

Revelation and the Word of God Because the book of Revelation forms part of the Bible, we know that it belongs to God's Word to us. Revelation enjoys the divine attributes of a Spirit-filled and -empowered body of writing, written to be read, understood, and obeyed (Rev. 1:3). Such an expectation appears in the instruction to John to write what he sees, and to send it to the seven churches in Asia (verse 11). We recognize this in the repeated refrain "He who has an ear, let him hear what the Spirit says to the churches" (Rev. 2:7, 11, 17, 29; 3:6, 13, 22). The first angel's summons to "every nation and tribe and tongue and people" (Rev. 14:6) states it. And we find it clearly expressed in the book's closing invitation and warning (Rev. 22:17-19).

Revelation reflects the author's sense of urgency. The end-time is near (Rev. 1:3), the Second Advent is about to take place (Rev. 22:10, 12, 20). Our response to the three angels' proclamations (Rev. 14:6-11) will determine the destiny of peoples and nations. And it is a time of great conflict and tribulation, a time for God's people to respond with courage (verse 12) under the lordship of the risen Christ.

Thus we must read the book of Revelation with this expectation and urgency if we are to understand it at all. We must approach it with a mind open to the Spirit's influence, and with a readiness to respond in gratitude and obedience to what Christ has done for us and will do for us in the glorious future about to break in upon us. As divine revelation, the book demands and anticipates that its readers will obey its summons "The Spirit and the Bride say, 'Come.' And let him who hears say, 'Come.' And let him who is thirsty come, let him who desires take the water of life without price" (Rev. 22:17).

The Revelation of Jesus Christ (Rev. 1:1-3) The book

begins with the words "The revelation of Jesus Christ," meaning a revelation given or mediated by Jesus Christ rather than about Himself. The Greek allows both interpretations, but the context indicates that the revelation has more to do with events that will transpire during the last days. Jesus gave the revelation "to show . . . what must soon take place" (verse 1). In the Greek original, the word rendered "revelation" is *apokalupsis*, which is made up of the words *apo*, meaning "away from," and *kalupsis*, "a veiling." We may translate *apokalupsis*, then, as "an unveiling." The book of Revelation is an unveiling of last things or events. The truth it contains comes to us, not from human discovery, but from divine disclosure.

But it would be incorrect to suggest that the book limits itself to last things and events. It presents a picture of Jesus, as well, a portrait unique to the book. For here we find a vision of the exalted Christ in high priestly and royal apparel (verses 12-16), depicted in symbolic imagery as a Lamb with seven horns and seven eyes (Rev. 5:6) and as an all-powerful conquering Messiah (Rev. 19:11-16). And in the letters to the seven churches, the message of the risen Lord is as much a self-disclosure by Jesus as it is a revelation of God's will and purpose to Christians.

The book has a twofold purpose: 1. It seeks *to inform* the believers about the dark trials awaiting them, enabling them to prepare for the tough times ahead and thus ride out the storm of controversy triumphantly. This is the way God works. He does not deceive us or mislead us about the future. The enlightenment God brings to the church illumines our understanding of our true condition, as well. We then can change what is necessary. God does not leave us to fight against Satan or to have to resist his temptations and avoid his entanglements in ignorance and weakness. When God unveils the future, He exposes the devil's schemes, sheds light on the course of action to take, and opens our eyes to the resources He has made available to us in Jesus.

2. It has as its purpose *to encourage* the church to hold fast until Christ returns, to endure the tribulation with patience and tenacity, and to be faithful at all costs, even to death. Historians today recognize the battle of Iwo Jima as one of the most important American victories of World War II. It was also one of the bloodiest engagements in modern military history. With its vast system of tunnels and underground fortifications, Iwo Jima became an incredible fortress, compelling the Americans to pay

dearly for every foot of ground. On March 23, 1945, about five o'clock in the afternoon, a Japanese radioman sent the message "All officers and men of Chichi Hima, goodbye". [1] The army officer telling the story recalled his weeping that afternoon as he thought of the gallantry of that radioman. The soldier held his position until death took him.

The book of Revelation begins with a brief but terse statement of how God transmits His message to us. The process begins with God, the source of all truth. Whenever a revelation occurs, it takes place because God has chosen to make truth known. Revealed truth is therefore a manifestation of God's holy will and a disclosure of His saving purpose. It is for our benefit that He makes it known to us.

When God opens His will to us, He does it through Jesus. The fourth Gospel declares Jesus to be the Word through whom God created everything (John 1:1-4), the light that enlightens everyone (verse 9), one in whom grace and truth resided fully (verse 14). Jesus Himself stated that He is "the way, and the truth, and the life" (John 14:6). He is not one way among many, but *the* only way to the Father: "No one comes to the Father, but by me" (verse 6). If we know Jesus, we know also the Father (verse 7). The author of Hebrews tells us that Jesus reflects God's glory and "bears the very stamp of his nature" (Heb. 1:3). Jesus is thus more than the bearer of God's word—He is the very embodiment of it. In the person and work of Jesus, God disclosed Himself fully. The truth that Jesus brings to us from God is the light and life made possible through His saving death and resurrection. It is the risen Lord, the exalted Christ who imparts to us God's saving truth.

In turn Jesus sends the message to John through His angel (Rev. 1:1; 22:16). The word "angel" is a Greek one (*aggelos*, pronounced an-ge-los with a hard g) meaning "one sent" or "messenger." Jesus made known to John the revelation God gave Him by *dispatching* His angel, or messenger.

In apocalyptic literature, such as Daniel and Revelation, angels play a prominent role in the revelatory process. Gabriel explains the significance of the vision to Daniel (Dan. 8:15-26), and comes to the prophet in answer to prayer to give him "wisdom and understanding" (Dan. 9:20-23).

Angels abound in the book of Revelation. Heaven assigned angels to the seven churches in Asia (Rev. 2 and 3). Four angels stand at the four corners of the earth, holding back the four winds (Rev. 7:1). Seven angels stand before God, seven trumpets are given them, and they prepare to blow (Rev. 8:2, 6). John sees another angel ministering before the golden altar of incense in the heavenly sanctuary (verses 3-5). A mighty angel with a little scroll in his hand straddles the sea and the land (Rev. 10:1, 2). Three angels issue the divine summons to all the world's inhabitants (Rev. 14:6-11). Another angel exits the temple with a sharp sickle in his hand, indicating imminent judgment (verses 17-20). Seven angels await to pour out the seven last plagues upon the wicked (Rev. 15:1). An angel with great authority announces God's last warning to His people, and another angel appeals to them to come out of Babylon (Rev. 18:1-4). The angel with the key to the bottomless pit and a great chain seizes the devil and locks him up for a thousand years (Rev. 20:1-3).

Still another angel bears a message from Jesus to John (Rev. 1:1; 22:16). When the prophet attempts to worship the divine messenger, the angel warns, "You must not do that! I am a fellow servant with you and your brethren who hold the testimony of Jesus. Worship God" (Rev. 19:10; cf. Rev. 22:8, 9).

John thus receives the revelation from the angel and puts it in writing, referring to himself as Christ's servant. The Greek New Testament has two words for "servant." 1. *Diakonos,* from which our word "deacon" comes, may be translated as "one who renders service to another." The apostle Paul uses *diakonos* in reference to the work of the gospel ministry (1 Cor. 3:5; 1 Tim. 4:6). The same word appears in the book of Acts in connection with the preaching ministry and evangelistic activity of Stephen and Philip (Acts 6-8).

2. The second word is *doulos,* which may be rendered as "slave." A *doulos* was one bound to servitude by economic or political circumstances. The word represents service under restraint. John employs it to refer to himself and his fellow believers (Rev. 1:1). His angel uses it to speak of himself (Rev. 19:10; 22:9). The prophet does not mean that he was drafted into the Lord's service against his will and compelled to write to the churches. Instead, he chose the word because it described more pointedly the circumstances under which he found himself forced to work because of his faithful witness to Jesus. He willingly suffered for Christ's sake, and with gratitude considered himself Christ's slave. Revelation's author preferred imprisonment under the most oppressive conditions to a life of ease won through compromise.

As a willing, loving slave, John testifies "to the word of God and to the testimony of Jesus Christ" (Rev. 1:2), that is, to "the revelation of Jesus Christ" (verse 1), the disclosure that God gave to Jesus and that reaches John from Jesus through the angel. It is at the same time a revelation that comes through a vision. The prophet says that he bears witness to "all that he saw" (verse 2). Words denoting visual and audio communication and perception appear frequently in the book, indicating that John intended his book as an eyewitness report. [2]

The divine revelation was written to benefit the church: "Blessed is he who reads aloud the words of the prophecy, and blessed are those who hear, and who keep what is written therein; for the time is near" (verse 3). The threefold blessing includes: 1. The blessing that comes from reading God's Word. John refers to the common custom in early Jewish and Christian services to have a designated person read the Scriptures publicly. Luke tells us of one occasion when Jesus recited from the Isaiah scroll in the presence of the congregation (Luke 4:16-19), and of another time when the apostle Paul received an invitation to speak after a public reading of the Bible (Acts 13:15).

2. The blessing that results from listening to God's Word. It takes place when the congregation has assembled for public worship. The book of Hebrews instructs us to "hold fast the confession of our hope" and to not neglect to meet together, but to "stir up one another to love and good works" and encourage one another as we see "the Day drawing near" (Heb. 10:23-25). The revelation of Jesus Christ is a message directed to the entire church, and therefore must be read and heard by the entire body. God did not give it for private interpretation (see 2 Peter 1:19-21).

3. The blessing that comes from obeying God's Word. In the Hebrew language, one of the words for "to hear" also means "to obey." Those who disobeyed had refused to listen to God's instruction (Jer. 13:15-17). Jesus told His disciples that He taught in parables in order to reveal the mysteries of God's kingdom to those who had ears to hear (Matt. 13:10-17). He was speaking of the receptivity of a person's mind, the readiness to respond positively to revealed truth. James tells us that the blessing results, not from merely listening and then forgetting, but from the action taken in response to the divine instruction (James 1:22-25).

In his book John uses the word *akouo*, which means "to heed" or "mark attentively." When my father wanted to get the attention of my three brothers and me, he would begin by saying, "Mark my words." It sounded ominous to us, so we sat still and took notice. John tells us to mark his words, for "the time is near" (Rev. 1:3). We mark something so that we will remember it, and to emphasize its importance. When studying for an examination, students will underline textbook statements that they should know for the test. Underlining is a learning device that helps them commit the information to memory.

God gave the revelation of Jesus Christ "to show . . . what must soon take place" (verse 1). John says "the time is near." What he refers to here is the time of the prophesied events, the end-time. The revelation has to do with events that are about to transpire, bringing an end to world history and the return of Christ. This viewpoint shapes the entire content of the book and creates a sense of urgency to the believers.

When my wife and I married, we did so with a hope that we could have children. When she became pregnant, our hope changed to expectation. The pregnancy made the difference between belief and conviction. Not only did we believe that we were going to have a child but we knew it, and took steps to prepare for the event. John writes with the certainty of conviction. The time of Christ's return is near. The tribulations facing the church were and are the birth pangs of the coming kingdom. We do well, therefore, to mark the words of this prophecy!

The Greeting to the Seven Churches in Asia (Rev. 1:4-8)
The book of Revelation is apocalyptic prophecy, but John introduces it as a letter to the seven churches in Asia. The literary form is standard, similar to the letters of Paul and other New Testament writers (for example, see Rom. 1:1, 7; 1 Cor. 1:1-3; Gal. 1:1-5). The salutation has the typical mention of grace and peace, the common Christian greeting that expressed a wish for God's blessing upon the readers. The word "grace" refers to the divine resources God makes available to the believer in Christ. It has to do with God's act of forgiveness in Jesus, which releases us from bondage in sin and binds us to a relationship with Him. *Peace* points to the benefits we enjoy in our new relationship with Him. No longer do we live in a state of animosity and estrangement, but in one of reconciliation to God (Romans 5:1-5). Our new relationship entitles us to free access to the Father to receive continual help in our pilgrimage of faith. The word "peace" means more than the absence of conflict. It depicts the privileged status of the believer in Christ.

The greeting continues with unusual titles of the Trinity: 1. First, we find the reference to God as "him who is and who was and who is to come" (Rev. 1:4), a restatement of the divine name I AM (see Ex. 3:14) and serving to stress the changeless nature or eternal presence of God. As a designation of a deity, the title was not uncommon in New Testament times. The pagan Greeks spoke of "Zeus who was, Zeus who is, and Zeus who will be." [3] Jewish rabbis interpreted the divine name in Exodus 3:14 to mean "I was; I still am; and in the future I will be." [4] And in Hebrews 13:8 we read that "Jesus Christ is the same yesterday and today and for ever." John's reference to God's changelessness sought to strengthen the believers as they faced persecution. The same God who delivered the Hebrew slaves from the oppressive hands of the Egyptians would go before the Christians, leading them through the tribulation to the kingdom.

2. Next, we have a description of the Holy Spirit as "the seven spirits who are before his throne" (Rev. 1:4). The expression "seven spirits" occurs in three other places in the book (Rev. 3:1; 4:5; 5:6), but nowhere else in the New Testament. Any attempt to interpret the phrase must take into account the significance of the number seven for John. The fact that it appears often in connection with other subjects indicates that we should understand it symbolically. [5] Viewed as such, the number seven, then, signifies completeness or perfection. That "seven spirits" refers to the Holy Spirit is an assumption we make from the context of Revelation 1:4. In none of the salutations of the New Testament Epistles do we find a blessing from the Holy Spirit. Instead, the writings of the apostle Paul repeatedly refer to God the Father and the Lord Jesus Christ (Rom. 1:7; 1 Cor. 1:3; 2 Cor. 1:2; Gal. 1:3; Eph. 1:2; Phil. 1:2; 1 Thess. 1:1; 2 Thess. 1:2; 1 Tim. 1:2; 2 Tim. 1:2; Titus 1:4; and Phil. 1:3).

In the book of Revelation, the "seven spirits" appear before God's throne and have a special role in connection with the Lamb. We may best understand the plurality of the Spirit in the context of Christ's revelatory work. As mentioned before, the revelation of Jesus Christ has to do with God's message to the church about last-day events. And Jesus mediates it to John. But when the human prophet relates to us the vision of the risen Lord, he tells us that he was "in the Spirit" (Rev. 1:10). [6]

It is the Spirit who opens the eyes of the seer and enables him to understand the vision. Moreover, in each of Christ's messages to the seven churches, we find the exhortation "He who has an ear, let him hear what the Spirit says to the churches" (Rev. 2:7, 11, 17, 29; 3:6, 13, 22). The Holy Spirit has a special ministry to perform in the churches, but we must not understand it as something separate from that of our risen Lord. The Spirit illumines the minds of the believers and empowers them in preparation for the impending tribulation. We may see the expression "seven spirits," then, as signifying the universal operation of the Spirit in the full ministry of the church. The Spirit manifests Himself in each of the seven churches for both their enlightenment and strengthening.

3. Third, we encounter a threefold designation of Jesus: a. He is "the faithful witness" (Rev. 1:5), a title denoting the reliability or trustworthy character of the testimony of Jesus. Jesus is the faithful witness because He is God's Son and can speak the truth about God as no one else can. Whereas the law arrived through Moses, John tells us, grace and *truth* came through Jesus Christ (John 1:17). As the Word who was with God, Jesus was the full embodiment of saving truth. Others may bear witness to truth, but Jesus alone could say I am the truth (John 14:6). He entered the world to bear witness to divine truth (John 18:37), and through His perfect life and sacrificial death He testified to it. While the title Faithful Witness refers primarily to Christ's testimony concerning the revelation He received from His Father (the contents of the book of Revelation), it has a broader meaning that includes the witness Jesus bore throughout His earthly ministry. He was faithful even to the point of death.

b. He is "the first-born of the dead" (Rev. 1:5). We may see the phrase as a reference to the resurrection of Jesus. He is firstborn, not in a chronological sense, but as a matter of priority. John here designates the primacy and preeminence of Christ's resurrection. The expression "firstborn" also brings to mind the Old Testament custom of the birthright (see Gen. 27:1-40). The firstborn enjoyed a position of prominence in his father's house and was heir to his father's possessions. The apostle Paul applies the title Firstborn of the dead to Christ (Col. 1:18) to emphasize His sovereignty in the church. The word "firstborn" appears in a Messianic psalm as well: "I will make him the first-born, the highest of the kings of the earth" (Ps. 89:27). The psalm also speaks of the King as God's "faithful one" (verse 19). The title thus denotes Christ's supreme sovereignty in the world by virtue of His faithfulness to God.

c. He is "the ruler of the kings on earth" (Rev. 1:5). The

expression attests to the defeat Christ handed the devil in the wilderness (Matt. 4:1-11), and ultimately through His death and resurrection. As firstborn of the dead, Jesus was declared ruler. The title Ruler of kings alludes to Psalm 89:27 and anticipates the supreme appellation at the end of time when Jesus will be acknowledged King of kings and Lord of lords (see Rev. 17:14; 19:16). Jesus' threefold title thus serves to encourage those facing martyrdom to endure the tribulation, for the way to the kingdom is the road of the cross.

Next, John introduces us to a doxology to Jesus that recites His saving deeds on our behalf: 1. He "loves us and has freed us from our sins" (Rev. 1:5). Of interest are the tenses of the verbs. The first is in the present tense to indicate Christ's unceasing love for us. His earthly ministry and sacrificial death manifested that love in the past. And His ministry in the heavenly sanctuary as our high priest provides evidence that He continues to love us in the present. The second verb appears in the present perfect tense, signifying a completed action at the time of John's writing. At the cost of His life, Jesus freed us from our sins. John here has in mind Christ's death on the cross. It took place at a particular point in time, and that one act set us free.

2. Christ "made us a kingdom, priests to his God" (verse 6). The statement recalls God's promise to Israel at Mount Sinai (Ex. 19:6). On the condition of their obedience, God would make the Jewish people "a kingdom of priests and a holy nation." The early Christians saw the promise reach its fulfillment in Jesus. The apostle Peter thus writes to the believers, "You are a chosen race, a royal priesthood, a holy nation, God's own people" (1 Peter 2:9). Through His obedience to God, Jesus has established a new royal line and has exalted us to a preeminence with Him (see Eph. 4:6-8). The believer's royal standing appears in connection with Christ's exaltation as ruler over earthly kings. The reference to that blissful state anticipates the millennial reign of Christ. At that time God will raise to life those who suffered martyrdom "for their testimony to Jesus and for the word of God," and they will serve as priests of God in their thousand-year reign with Christ (Rev. 20:4, 6). Thus, in a corporate sense, they are a kingdom, while individually they serve as priests.

As the believers' royal status appears in connection with Christ's kingship, so their priestly role results from Christ's sacrifice and high priestly ministry. Through His victory over the evil powers, Christ opens a new way to God (Heb. 10:19-22), establishing a new priesthood of all believers. And as the new Israel of God, Christians enjoy direct access to God's presence and the privileged status associated with it—the tangible benefits of Christ's sacrificial death and resurrection!

John continues with more praise to Christ (Rev. 1:6). It consists of two things: 1. John ascribes glory to Jesus. The word "glory" here depicts the manifestation of God's presence. When Moses asked God to see His glory, the Lord replied, "I will make all my goodness pass before you, and will proclaim before you my name 'The Lord' " (Ex. 33:19). God discloses His glory through His mighty acts on behalf of His people, and at the same time He makes known His presence. Anciently God manifested His dwelling among His people by filling the tabernacle with His glory (Ex. 40:34-38). It was an awesome display of His holiness. In His high priestly prayer, Jesus pled for God to surround Him with the glory He had enjoyed in His preexistence as God's Son (John 17:5). Jesus receives glorification through His death, resurrection, and exaltation, and it involves the full participation of the Deity (Phil. 2:5-11). In the concluding section of the book of Revelation, John presents a beautiful thought: God will reveal His glory by dwelling in the midst of His people. The New Jerusalem will have no temple, nor need of sun or moon. Instead, the redeemed will walk in the light of Christ's glory (Rev. 21:3, 22-24).

2. John ascribes dominion to Jesus. The word "dominion," found in other New Testament ascriptions of praise to Jesus (1 Tim. 6:16; 1 Peter. 4:11; Jude 25), depicts the supreme sovereignty of the risen Christ. It is a rulership made evident in His triumph over the evil powers through His death and resurrection, and one that all will fully acknowledge at or around the time of His second coming (Rev. 6:15-17; 7:9-12; 11:15-18; 15:3, 4; 19:1-7).

The words "glory" and "dominion" thus point to the priestly and royal aspects of Christ's work. He is both a royal priest and a priestly king in that He intercedes for His people by virtue of His blood and reigns over them through His conquest of Satan and his evil forces. In a very real sense His glory and dominion are bound inseparably to His relationship with us: He is glorified to the extent that His sovereign will finds expression in our corporate life and witness. John's ascription of praise to Jesus is at the same time a prayer that Christ truly will be exalted and glorified in the church.

A prophecy of Christ's return follows the doxology (Rev. 1:7). Both a promise and a warning, it brings hope to those under the

pressure of persecution, and awakens dread among the enemies
of God's people. John's prophetic statement tells us four things:
1. Christ returns "with the clouds." The text directs us to
Daniel's vision of the Son of man coming to the Ancient of days
(Daniel 7:13). Some commentators see significance in the prepo-
sition *with*, suggesting that the biblical writer envisions the Son
of man as compelling "all the clouds into His retinue." [7] In the
apocalyptic prophecy in Matthew, the Son of man arrives *on* the
clouds (Matt. 24:30), and in Mark's Gospel, He appears *in* clouds
(Mark 13:26). [8] It is clear that the New Testament writers drew
from the language and imagery of Daniel, but whether John
deliberately differs from the Gospel accounts to make a point is
not certain. He may be simply following more closely the
wording in the book of Daniel. In either case, the phrase "with
the clouds" or "on the clouds" or "in the clouds" signifies the
transcendent glory and sovereignty of the Son of man. During
Israel's wandering in the wilderness, the cloud represented
God's presence (Ex. 13:21; 40:34-38). Matthew tells us that when
Jesus was transfigured, a "bright cloud overshadowed" Peter,
James, and John, and that from the cloud God spoke to the eye
witnesses (Matt. 17:1, 2, 5). What John wants us to understand is
that the second advent of Jesus will be the time when the exalted
Christ will appear with God in the full splendor and majesty of
heaven. And that His glorious appearance signals the end of
human history and the beginning of the new age.

2. Everyone will witness Christ's return. The Second Advent
is a public event, not a private experience. The passage rules out
the notion of a secret rapture, by which God mysteriously
transports believers to heaven. Here John is consistent with
Paul's view of Christ's coming as an event proclaimed "with a cry
of command, with the archangel's call, and with the sound of the
trumpet of God" (1 Thess. 4:16). There will be no mistake as to its
occurrence.

3. Those who pierced Jesus will witness His return. The
fourth Gospel relates the incident of a Roman soldier thrusting a
spear into the side of Jesus, an unnecessary act because Jesus
was dead, a fact that the soldiers already recognized (John 19:33,
34). The fourth Gospel views the incident as a fulfillment of the
Messianic prophecy in Zechariah 12:10. The prophet Zechariah
envisions a restoration of the royal house of David, accompanied
by the nation's repentance for their rejection and abusive treatment of God's Anointed One (see verses 10-14). John in Revelation

adapts the passage to suit his own purpose. The expression "every one who pierced him" extends beyond the actual episode at the time of Christ's crucifixion and includes all those who had an active part in Christ's death as well as those who have risen up against the followers of Jesus (see Acts 9:1-9).

4. All the wicked will mourn when they witness the return of Jesus. The reference to the tribes of the earth mourning at the second coming of Jesus occurs in the Gospel of Matthew as well, and represents an adaptation of the Messianic prophecy of Zechariah (Matthew 24:30; Zech. 12:10-14). In Revelation the mourning of the tribes of the earth appears in striking contrast to the rejoicing among God's people. The wailing of the wicked as a counterpart to the joy of the righteous is a theme that appears throughout the book (Rev. 6:15-17 and 7:9-12; 11:13 and verses 15-18; 18:9-19 and verse 20), and serves to bolster the spirits of believers awaiting the dark hour of conflict.

John concludes the salutation with a threefold description of God (Rev. 1:8): 1. He is the Alpha and the Omega. *Alpha* is the first letter of the Greek alphabet, and *omega* the last. The phrase or its equivalent occurs also in Revelation 21:6 and 2:8, and indicates the absolute completeness of God. He is the first and the last, the one who initiates and brings to completion what He wills to do. In his letter to the Philippians, Paul writes, "I am sure that he who began a good work in you will bring it to completion at the day of Jesus Christ" (Phil. 1:6). The book of Hebrews calls Jesus "the pioneer and perfecter of our faith" (Heb. 12:2; the KJV reads "the author and finisher"). "I am the Alpha and the Omega" forms an appropriate conclusion to the Revelation 1:7 prophecy of Christ's second advent, and reminds the believers that God has the first and last word in human affairs, and therefore determines the course of history.

2. God is one who lives in the eternal present. The phrase "who is and who was and who is to come" stresses the changelessness of God, and hence the reliability of His Word. The believers can place their confidence in the revelation given to them, for the One who controls the course of history has disclosed to them "what must soon take place" (Rev. 1:1).

(3) He is the Almighty. The title is a favorite of John, appearing eight times in the book. When interpreted in the context of the two other designations, it points to the unchallenged sovereignty and superiority of the Deity. The oppression of Rome will soon give way to the supremacy of God, who alone is almighty!

[1] Richard Wheeler, *Iwo*, pp. 210, 211.

[2] See *The SDA Bible Commentary*, vol. 7, p. 730.

[3] As quoted by Robert H. Mounce, in *The New International Commentary on the New Testament: The Book of Revelation*, p. 68.

[4] In William Barclay, *The Revelation of John*, rev. ed., vol. 1, p. 29.

[5] See *The SDA Bible Commentary*, vol. 7, p. 737.

[6] See also Revelation 17:3: "And he carried me away in the Spirit into a wilderness."

[7] Mounce, p. 72.

[8] Paul speaks of the believers as being taken up with the resurrected saints "in the clouds" at the second coming of Christ (1 Thess. 4:17).

A Vision of
the Risen Lord

(Based on Revelation 1:9-20)

"The Lord is my light and my salvation;
whom shall I fear?
The Lord is the stronghold of my life;
of whom shall I be afraid?" (Ps. 27:1).

Tribulation and the Kingdom (Rev. 1:9-11)   In the introductory vision John refers to himself by the affectionate title "your brother" (verse 9), thus testifying to the spiritual bonding among Christian believers. He calls attention to three things they share together in Christ: (1) the tribulation, (2) the kingdom, and (3) the patient endurance. The tribulation is the suffering Rome meted out to John as payment for his Christian witness, and the persecution that his fellow believers were facing as well. It came as no surprise. Jesus had predicted it (John 16:33), the apostles had already experienced it (see Acts 12:1-5), and they had taught the rest of the believers to expect it (see 2 Tim. 3:12).

The way to the kingdom is the road of tribulation—not suffering in general, but the persecution one encounters for his or her faith. "Kingdom" refers to the coming reign of Christ that commences at the Second Advent, the event that brings the tribulation to a decisive end. *Patient endurance* forms the hallmark of the Christians' faith. In the original Greek of the book it is *hupomone*, that spiritual quality that enables the believer to cling tenaciously to the blessed hope in Jesus, and move forward into the arena of hostile forces with a spirit of courage and gallantry.

Throughout the New Testament we find an emphasis on patient endurance. Jesus instructs the disciples accordingly: "He who endures to the end will be saved" (Matt. 24:13). One time Paul and Barnabas were exhorting the new converts "to continue in the faith, and saying that through many tribulations [they] must enter the kingdom of God" (Acts 14:22). Peter reminds his readers that tribulation tests and proves their faith (1 Peter 1:6, 7;

4:12), and James adds that such testing develops *hupomone*, (James 1:3), enabling them to move from victory to victory in Christ.

In the book of Revelation, John follows his portrayal of the persecution awaiting Christians for their faith with a call for patient endurance (Rev. 13:10; 14:12). It is a summons to resist the pagan pressure to compromise, and—if necessary—to resist to the death.

For the present, John's punishment consisted of banishment to the desolate island of Patmos, a penal colony established by Rome. [1] Some believe exile was not the only price he paid for his faith. William Ramsay speaks of John's banishment being "preceded by scourging, and it was marked by perpetual fetters, scanty clothing, insufficient food, sleep on the bare ground in a dark prison, and work under the lash of military overseers." [2] William Barclay reasons that the Roman authorities treated the prophet as a criminal and therefore sentenced him to hard labor in the local quarries. [3]

The tribulation that he endured opened his soul to God and prepared him for the revelation he received in exile. John does not focus attention on his suffering. He simply tells us that he had been banished to the island of Patmos because of his witness to "the word of God and the testimony of Jesus" (Rev. 1:9). In such a setting and in such circumstances, John receives his commission to write (verse 11). The rugged terrain surrounded by miles of ocean (the Aegean Sea) undoubtedly gave rise to the language and imagery of the book. When John describes the wicked seeking refuge in the caves and rocks of the mountains at the second advent of Christ (Rev. 6:15-17), or the beast rising out of the sea (Rev. 13:1), he may well have thought of his immediate environment. [4] The word *thalassa*, translated "sea," appears 26 times in the book. And, as one writer observes: "nowhere is the 'voice of many waters' (Rev. 14:2; 19:6, KJV) more musical than in Patmos; nowhere does the rising and setting sun make a more splendid 'sea of glass mingled with fire' (Rev. 15:2); yet nowhere is the longing more natural that the separating sea should be no more." [5]

John testifies that the Roman authorities had banished him to Patmos "on account of the word of God and the testimony of Jesus." By the phrase "word of God," he has in mind not only the content of the revelation given to him, but also the Old Testament, particularly as it finds fulfillment in Jesus. So much of the book of Revelation is in fact saturated with references to the Hebrew Scriptures, whether in the form of quotations or as allusions. The "testimony of Jesus" is not only Christ's confirmation of the revelation God imparts to John, but also Christ's witness to the truth regarding His Father, a faithful witness manifested in His life and teachings (John 17:3, 4).[6]

The exiled prophet's vision of the exalted Christ and his commission to write remind us of the religious experience of Isaiah and Ezekiel. Both began their prophetic ministries with a vision of God's glory (Isa. 6:1-5; Eze. 1). John states that he was "in the Spirit" and he heard behind him "a loud voice like a trumpet" (Rev. 1:10). He wants us to understand that the revelation came to him, not from his own inner thoughts, but from the outer manifestation of the Holy Spirit. It was an awesome and wonderful experience, similar to the revelation of the law at Sinai: "There were thunders and lightnings, and a thick cloud upon the mountain, and a very loud trumpet blast" (Ex. 19:16).

John's vision of Jesus came to him on the "Lord's day" (Rev. 1:10), an expression occurring only once in the New Testament, and thereby giving rise to much speculation. Contrary to the opinion of many Christian writers, the words "Lord's day" cannot here refer to Sunday worship, since we lack biblical evidence that such an institution existed in the Christian community during the first century. And the prophet writes as though his readers, grounded in the faith, would know precisely the day to which he referred. It is more reasonable to understand "Lord's day" as referring to the Sabbath of the fourth commandment.

John certainly knew of the Sabbath controversies between Jesus and the Pharisees, and of Christ's claim to be Lord of the Sabbath (Matt. 12:1-8). Moreover, the prophet describes the people of God as "those who keep the commandments of God" (Rev. 12:17; 14:12). It makes no sense if the Christians to whom he wrote were living in violation of the fourth commandment and in complete disregard to the claim that Jesus makes of being Lord of that day.

It was on the Sabbath, then, that John received his vision and commission. The commission was a command to write and to send what he had composed to seven specific churches in Asia Minor: those in Ephesus, Smyrna, Pergamum, Thyatira, Sardis, Philadelphia, and Laodicea (Rev. 1:11). The order in which Revelation addresses the churches is a geographical one. They were literal congregations situated along a well-traveled Roman road.[7] A messenger bearing the scroll of Revelation would begin at Ephesus, the church closest to the island of Patmos, and would proceed northward on the imperial road to Smyrna and then to Pergamum, after which he would head in a southeasterly direction to Thyatira, Sardis, Philadelphia, and Laodicea.

The Vision of Jesus (Rev. 1:12-16)   John in vision sees the risen Lord in the holy splendor of a high priest and in the royal majesty of a triumphant king. The prophet develops his picture by drawing from a variety of Old Testament passages.

1. Jesus appears in the midst of seven golden lampstands (verses 12, 13). The language and imagery here form a composite picture derived from three passages: (a) the depiction of the seven-lamped stand of pure gold that God told Moses to make for the wilderness sanctuary (Ex. 25:31-37); (b) the mention of the 10 golden lampstands in the Temple of Solomon (1 Kings 7:49); and (c) Zechariah's vision of a golden lampstand with "a bowl on the top of it, and seven lamps on it" (Zech. 4:2). Both in the wilderness sanctuary and in the Temple of Solomon the lampstands served the practical purpose of providing light (see Ex. 39:37), whereas the candlestick with seven lamps in Zeachariah's vision had a symbolic meaning. An angel explains to the prophet that the seven lamps represent "the eyes of the Lord, which range through the whole earth" (Zech. 4:10). In Revelation the seven lampstands signify the seven churches of Asia (Rev. 1:20).

The picture of Jesus in the midst of the lampstands points to Christ's continuing presence and activity on behalf of the church in His exalted role as high priest. The risen Lord presents the needs and concerns of the churches to His Father, and reveals God's holy will and redemptive purpose to the churches. Christ's intercessory activity enables the church to fulfill its light-bearing function in the world.

2. Jesus appears as "one like a son of man" (verse 13). The language reminds the reader of scenes from the books of Daniel and Ezekiel. The prophet Daniel sees in a nighttime vision "one like a son of man" coming with the clouds of heaven and being presented to the Ancient of days to receive the kingdom (Dan. 7:13, 14). The picture of the transcendent Son of man contrasts sharply with the defeated bestial rulers and signifies the transfer of dominion from the earthly monarchs to the Messiah. In Ezekiel, "Son of man" title refers to the prophet himself (Eze. 2:1, 3, 6, 8; 3:1, 3, 4, 10, 17, 25; and so on). Jesus frequently used the

phrase to express His awareness of having to fulfill God's plan for His life (Matt. 12:8; 13:37; Luke 19:10). That plan consisted of His humiliation through His identification with sinful humankind (Matt. 8:20; 11:19), the culmination of which took place on the cross (Matt. 17:12; 20:18), and His exaltation, beginning with His resurrection and becoming fully manifested at the time of the Second Advent (Matt. 13:41; 24:27, 30; 25:31).[8]

"Son of man" occurs twice in the book of Revelation. Besides being in the introductory vision, it appears in the judgment scene that follows the warning messages of the three angels (Rev. 14:14). Both passages in Revelation clearly depict the exalted role of the risen Lord as judge over all the earth. In the introductory vision, Christ's position of preeminence in the universe follows His defeat of the rulers of this world by means of His death and resurrection.

3. He wears "a long robe and . . . a golden girdle round his breast" (Rev. 1:13). The image brings to mind the clothing of the Old Testament high priest (Ex. 28:4; 29:5; Lev. 16:4), and in this way points to the high priestly character of Christ's present work. The Jewish historian Josephus describes the garments worn by the high priest who served in the Temple as a long robe that reached to the feet, with a girdle wound around the body above the elbows.[9] But we have evidence indicating that princes and kings also wore such clothing (1 Sam. 18:4; 24:5, 11; Eze. 26:16). The imagery thus directs our attention as well to the royal nature of Christ's present function (Rev. 17:14; 19:16). In addition, we note that the Divine Figure in Daniel's vision wears linen with a golden girdle (Dan. 10:5). He is a messenger from God whose purpose in coming to Daniel is to reveal the meaning of the vision. John depicts the seven angels with the seven plagues as robed in "pure bright linen, and their breasts girded with golden girdles" (Rev. 15:6). They are divine messengers about to implement God's judgment of wrath on the wicked. It is possible to see in this Revelation 1:13 description of the risen Lord, then, an allusion to Christ's role of divine revealer, as one bringing the message of God to John. Barclay views the passage as a reference to Christ's prophetic work, and concludes that the clothing portrays the risen Lord in His threefold office as prophet, priest, and king.[10]

4. His head and hair are white as wool, as snow (Rev. 1:14). The language derives from Daniel's description of the Ancient of days, whose clothing is white as snow and whose hair is like pure

wool (Dan. 7:9). It is possible that the color white represents age and purity, but more likely it conveys the idea of wisdom and dignity, since the setting in Daniel is one of judgment before the heavenly tribunal. Applied to Jesus, these divine attributes emphasize His exalted nature and work by virtue of His death and resurrection. A host of angels proclaim the wisdom of the Lamb (Rev. 5:12) and of God (Rev. 7:12). It is the attribute needed for understanding the mysteries in the book of Revelation (see Rev. 13:18; 17:9). The themes that appear the most important in the book, and that come to the forefront in the introductory vision, are Christ's worthiness, high rank, and preeminence, rather than His preexistence and sinlessness. [11]

5. His eyes are like a flame of fire (Rev. 1:14). The imagery appears again in the message to the church in Thyatira (Rev. 2:18), where the exalted Christ "searches mind and heart" (verse 23) and metes out judgment on the merits of each individual case. We find this description of His eyes also in the closing scenes in the book (Rev. 19:12), where the prophet again focuses on Christ's work of judgment (verse 11). And we note, as well, a similar description of the Divine Figure in the book of Daniel: "His eyes [were] like flaming torches" (Dan. 10:6; see Rev. 4:5).

The fiery eyes with the white head and hair solemnize the role of the risen Lord in and among the seven churches, and add emphasis to His status as faithful witness (Rev. 1:5). Nothing escapes His penetrating vision. His testimony is thus absolutely reliable and trustworthy (see Rev. 3:14; 19:11).

6. His feet are like polished brass. The text reads: "His feet were like burnished bronze, refined as in a furnace" (Rev. 1:15). We find similar expressions in Daniel 10:6, which depicts the arms and legs of the Divine Figure as "like the gleam of burnished bronze," and in Ezekiel 1:7, which describes the feet of heavenly beings as "like burnished bronze." The gleaming or sparkling indicates that the metal was treated with heat, a refining, or purging, process that would make it stronger. The description thus denotes strength and stability developed through the furnace of trial and affliction. [12]

7. His voice sounds like many waters (Rev. 1:15). H. B. Swete saw in the phrase an allusion to the sea surrounding the island of Patmos. [13] But the expression actually derives from Ezekiel 43:2: in the prophet's vision "the sound of many waters" announces the coming of the God of Israel. The words of the Divine Figure in Daniel's vision resemble "the noise of a multitude"

(Dan. 10:6). As a description of the risen Lord, this Revelation 1:15 phrase can have a twofold meaning: it may stand for the overpowering word of divine judgment or the soothing comfort of divine consolation, depending on the situation in the church.

8. He holds seven stars in His right hand (verse 16). Revelation 1:20 tells us that the seven stars in Christ's right hand represent the seven angels of the seven churches of Asia. There may be an allusion here to the prophetic passages of Isaiah that speak of God's incomparability. He measures the waters in "the hollow of his hand" (Isa. 40:12), and will strengthen and uphold His people by His "victorious right hand" (Isa. 41:10). In the fourth Gospel we note Christ's promise that none of His followers shall perish, for no one will be able to snatch them out of His hand (John 10:28). The picture of the exalted Christ holding the seven stars in His right hand assures the Christians under persecution that the earthly powers cannot alter God's plan for the church. Whatever the believers have to face, they can be certain that Christ will sustain them by the might of His right hand.

9. A sharp two-edged sword issues from His mouth (Rev. 1:16). Throughout the Bible we find references to God's word as a weapon of offense. Isaiah speaks of God smiting the earth with "the rod of his mouth" (Isa. 11:4), and of Him making the prophet's mouth "like a sharp sword" (Isa. 49:2). The apostle Paul labels the Word of God "the sword of the Spirit" (Eph. 6:17). Hebrews 4:12 calls God's Word "living and active, sharper than any two-edged sword." And in Revelation 19:15, John once again speaks of a sword issuing from the mouth of the risen Lord. The last instance presents Christ as the conquering Messiah going forth on His white horse to battle the forces of evil on earth (see verses 11-16).

The two-edged sword in the introductory vision of Christ, then, points to the penetrating power of God's Word. As an instrument of divine judgment, the sword issuing from Christ's mouth serves two purposes: First, it cuts through all human deception, laying bare our sin and exposing our need of God's grace. Second, it is the means by which the church militant becomes the church triumphant. Through the Word of God, the believers fight the enemy and conquer him (see Matt. 4:3-11).

10. His face shines like the sun in full strength (Rev. 1:16). It is possible that John here associates the brilliance depicted with the wisdom of the risen Lord (see Dan. 12:3), but more than likely,

he has in mind the scene at Christ's transfiguration (Matt. 17:2, 3, 5). John pictures the glorified Lord who leads His church through dark trials to the bright future awaiting the faithful. The expression concludes his description of the exalted Christ.

Next, John records the impact that the vision had on him, and the assurance that Jesus provides (Rev. 1:17, 18). It was a dreadfully wonderful experience, leaving the seer completely overwhelmed. He fell at Christ's feet as though dead. Daniel had the same experience after his vision of the Divine Figure (Dan. 10:9), as did Ezekiel when he saw the glory of the Lord (Eze. 1:28), and Peter, after the miraculous catch of fish (Luke 5:4-9). It was a manifestation of reverential awe that came in recognition of the majesty and splendor of the holiness of God.

On two other occasions John falls at the feet of the angel in an attitude of worship. The angel promptly forbids him to do so, telling him to worship God instead (Rev. 19:10; 22:8, 9).

Christ's response to the prostrated witness (see also Dan. 10:10; Matt. 17:6, 7) contains three additional descriptive titles:
1. "I am the first and the last, and the living one" (Rev. 1:17, 18). It expresses Christ's eternal nature. To be first and last means to have no one before and after Him. The title "the Living One" is a modification of the common Old Testament appellation "the living God" (Joshua 3:10; Ps. 42:2; 84:2), found also in the New Testament in reference to God the Father (Matt. 16:16; Acts 14:15; Heb. 10:31). As a designation of the risen Lord, "the Living One" stresses the absolute uniqueness of Jesus. The phrase contrasts the glorified Christ with the pagan gods, or more precisely those Roman emperors who declared themselves to be gods. Before there was a Roman Empire and long after it passed from the scene of human activity, there is Christ Jesus, the Living One. The believers should place their trust, therefore, in the eternal Christ, and not in transitory earthly powers.

The title says something reassuring about our relationship with Jesus. As the first and the last, He is always with us. There never was a time and there never will be a time in our experience without Him. He is the author and the finisher, the pioneer and the perfecter, of our faith (Heb. 12:2, KJV and RSV). The work that God began in us He will bring to completion at Christ's return (Phil. 1:6).

2. "I died, and behold I am alive for evermore" (Rev. 1:18). Jesus became a human being in order to suffer the death that sin destined each one of us to experience, and in so doing He paid

in full the penalty for us all. In this respect He went before us to prepare the way. His death is a fact of history that the most determined infidel cannot dispute. Beyond that, His life today as the risen Lord in our midst is a fact of faith that only the confirmed believer can proclaim! He died once for all, and lives forevermore.

With the tribulation looming before them, the believers took comfort in the fact that their Lord had traveled the way of suffering ahead of them, and had defeated the enemy. Death has thus lost its sting. While the enemy may exercise power over the body, he cannot touch the soul. The faithful can be certain of victory in Christ and go through the ordeal of persecution with the supreme confidence of entering into the eternal kingdom. Their death will be simply God's way of perfecting His plan in them.

3. "I have the keys of Death and Hades" (verse 18). In grim language the Old Testament pictures death and the grave as a prison house to which all must go and from which none can ever leave (see Ps. 9:13; 107:18; Isa. 38:10). Only the Lifegiver can unlock the gates of hell and set free the captives. By virtue of His death and resurrection Jesus has the authority and power to liberate His people from the prison house of sin. As an ascription of the risen Christ, the expression testifies to the fact that Jesus is now in charge of Death and Hades because of His victory over the evil forces. Consequently, they can no longer terrify the believer, since Jesus has "abolished death and brought life and immortality to light through the gospel" (2 Tim. 1:10). In the end Christ will cast Death and Hades into the lake of fire and throw away the keys (Rev. 20:14; 21:4).

Following these reassuring words, Christ once again commissions John to put in writing what he sees in vision (Rev. 1:19). The command ties the introductory vision to the messages to the seven churches. Christ explains to the prophet the meaning of the seven stars and the seven lampstands (verse 20) and in this way prepares the way for the instruction that follows. The stars represent the angels assigned to the individual churches. As such they are to be distinguished from the angel the risen Lord sent to assist John with the revelation (Rev. 1:1; 10:9; 19:9, 10; 22: 8, 9). The specified role of each of the seven angels is to bear the special message to the designated church.

As symbolic of the seven churches of Asia, the lampstands signify the role God expects the churches to play in His redemptive plan. He wants the churches to bring light to a world darkened by pagan beliefs and practices. The light they bear witnesses to the truth Jesus imparted to them through the gospel. In and of themselves they can provide no illumination. They can give light only to the extent that they have received it and are living in accordance with it.

---

[1] Eusebius informs us that John was among those released from exile following Domitian's reign. Eusebius refers to records from early Christian tradition as indicating that John resumed his residence in Ephesus (Ecclesiastical History 3. #20).

[2] William M. Ramsay, The Letters to the Seven Churches, p. 85.

[3] Barclay, The Revelation of John, rev. ed., vol. 1, p. 41.

[4] According to tradition, John wrote the book of Revelation from a cave in a cliff overlooking the sea. Near that site, the monk Christodulus founded the monastery of St. John in A.D. 1088 under the auspices of the emperor Alexius Comnenus (SDA Bible Dictionary, p. 843).

[5] In Barclay, pp. 41, 42.

[6] See J. R. Zurcher, Christ of the Revelation, p. 22.

[7] See Map XX in the SDA Bible Dictionary.

[8] For a fuller discussion of the significance of the title Son of man, see Oscar Cullmann, The Christology of the New Testament, p. 164.

[9] Josephus Antiquities of the Jews 3. 7. 2, 4.

[10] Barclay, p. 46.

[11] Against Barclay, p. 49.

[12] See J. M. Ford, Revelation, The Anchor Bible, p. 383.

[13] See Barclay, p. 50.

Messages to the
Seven Churches—I

(Based on Revelation 2)

"You are the light of the world. A city set on a hill cannot be hid. Nor do men light a lamp and put it under a bushel, but on a stand, and it gives light to all in the house" (Matt. 5:14, 15).

The Church in Ephesus (Rev. 2:1-7)   Established by the apostle Paul on his third missionary journey (Acts 19:1-10), the church in Ephesus grew rapidly, becoming a strong center of Christianity before the close of the first century. The light of truth then radiated to other Asian communities, under the able leadership and fervent witness of the local members. One writer observes: "Nowhere did the word of God find a kindlier soil, strike root more deeply or bear fairer fruits of faith and love." [1] We find among the early Christian workers there Aquila, Priscilla, and Apollos (Acts 18:18, 19, 24, 26). Timothy presided over the church as bishop some time after Paul founded it (see 1 Tim. 1:3). Later John assumed leadership and conducted his ministry in the heat of persecution until Rome sent him into exile. Christian legend tells of him bringing Mary, the mother of Jesus, to Ephesus, and of her dying and being buried there. [2] According to tradition, John died in Ephesus and was buried at the site where Christians later erected the Basilica of St. John. [3]

The city in which the church took root and flourished prospered from the trade and travel created by its great harbor, its location in the Cayster Valley, and the network of roads that connected Ephesus to major cities in Asia and Mesopotamia, as well as the trade route to Rome itself. [4] In John's day Ephesus became known as the Market of Asia, the gateway for merchants on their commercial journeys. In later years Christians passed through Ephesus on the way to their execution in Rome, and thus designated the city as the Highway of the Martyrs. [5]

Paganism with its superstitious belief in amulets and charms, and its sacred images and temples, thrived in the city. The great temple of Artemis (or Diana of the Ephesians; see Acts 19:23-41,

KJV) towered above the city, forming one of the seven wonders of the ancient world, and providing a refuge for fleeing criminals. Because of the hundreds of priestesses who served as temple prostitutes, Ephesus earned the reputation of being a center of immorality.[6] One commentator concludes: "It may be imagined how foul were the orgies sanctioned under such auspices, and, worst of all, sanctioned in the outraged name of religion."[7]

John introduces the message to the church with two descriptions of Jesus. As in the case with most of the seven churches, the descriptions derive from the introductory vision of Christ. The risen Lord comes to the church at Ephesus as one who holds the seven stars in His right hand, and who walks among the seven golden lampstands (Rev. 2:1). The picture reveals Christ's interest and unwearied activity on behalf of His church as a whole. Ellen White speaks of Christ's "constant diligence" and "eternal vigilance" as a model for church leaders to imitate: "He looks with intense interest to see whether His people are in such a condition spiritually that they can advance His kingdom."[8]

A depiction of the church follows next (verses 2-4). The members have worked hard and have demonstrated patient endurance for Christ's sake. But the congregation does have its faults. Christ complains that the members have abandoned their first love. However, He commends the church on three counts: (1) they have been zealous and diligent in their labors for the Lord, (2) they have been steadfast in the midst of tribulation, and (3) they have been vigilant, exposing evil men in the fellowship. But in the process of testing the saints and disciplining those guilty of heresy and apostasy, the congregation lost the loving characteristics of the gospel, the kind affection toward one another that set them apart from the pagans. They were correct in calling for discipline, but in the absence of love, they became self-righteous and legalistic in the way they administered it.

Christ follows His complaint with an admonition: "Remember then from what you have fallen, repent and do the works you did at first" (Acts 2:5). The counsel consists of three things: 1. The Christians are to remember, to recall the past in the light of the present so as to gain insight into their behavior. Such remembering will be possible through the Holy Spirit, and they can be sure that the Spirit will guide their thinking as long as they seek to respond to Christ's command. In the light of their new understanding, they will see the error of their ways and repent.

2. The word "repent" involves more than thinking through a problem. It has to do with action—specifically, change. We know when we have repented by the behavioral changes in our lives. Once we feel convinced of wrongdoing, we stop, make amends, and move in another direction.

Once after eating breakfast at a restaurant during a trip, I inadvertently took the northbound entrance to the interstate instead of the southbound. I traveled 20 miles in the opposite direction before I discovered my mistake, and had to continue an additional five miles before I reached an exit where I could get off the highway and change direction. During the last five miles I was frustrated, for I knew I had made a mistake, and I was eager to correct it. Once the Holy Spirit convicts us of sin and we are truly repentant, we will be motivated to change things as quickly as we can, and we will be miserable with every delay.

3. And finally, Christ says, "Do the works you did at first." The Christians have strayed from the path, and Jesus wants them to return and begin again. Starting over is important. And it is equally important to know that we can do so by God's grace, whether it be after failing in marriage, or flunking a college course, or suffering a personal tragedy. Repentance consists of change in direction and leads to renewal and growth.

In the event that the church fails to take His counsel to heart, Christ warns, "If not, I will come to you and remove your lampstand from its place" (verse 5). When there is no love in the fellowship, there can be no light in the world, and in time the church will die and its witness disappear from the community. Love in the church gives life and light to its message, because love is the energizing power of the Holy Spirit or the fruit in the life of the believer that enables him or her to nurture and edify one another.

But we must not separate love from truth and righteousness. Whenever that happens, love becomes sentimental, permissive, and powerless. So the risen Lord reminds the Ephesus Christians that their opposition toward the works of the Nicolaitans is commendable (verse 6). When it came to guarding the way of truth, the Ephesian church remained vigilant, testing all new teachers and firmly rejecting false doctrine and evil practices. References to such teachings and practices occur in the messages to the churches of Pergamum and Thyatira. Here we note that jealous love for the truth that refuses to tolerate error.

Two things now catch our attention: 1. We encounter

Christ's admonition "He who has an ear, let him hear what the Spirit says to the churches" (verse 7). Christ's sober invitation appears in each of the letters to the churches and emphasizes the need to pay attention to the message. The hour is late, the end comes quickly, and believers have no time for delay, doubt, or indifference.

2. We read Christ's promise of reward: "To him who conquers I will grant to eat of the tree of life, which is in the paradise of God" (verse 7). The reward of eternal life goes to the victor, to the one who conquers. The conquest, however, does not come simply by believers doing their best, by trying hard to overcome the enemy, since that would be impossible anyway. The apostle Paul reminds us that "we are more than conquerors through him who loved us" (Rom. 8:37), and that neither tribulation nor distress nor persecution nor famine nor nakedness nor peril nor sword can separate us from the love of Christ (verse 35). The believers' only hope of victory rests in their abiding in Christ's love.

The picture of the tree of life in the paradise of God originates in the story of Adam and Eve in the Garden of Eden. Among the Ephesian Christians the biblical image would stand in sharp contrast to the pagan beliefs and practices surrounding them. Sacred trees in pagan religion renewed the worshipers' strength. By feeding on the fruit of such trees, they believed they would receive the life-giving power of the gods. For the Christian the tree of life is not the means but the reward of victory. [9] What gives us power to overcome is a knowledge of the truth: "The knowledge that comes from God is the bread of life. It is the leaves of the tree of life which are for the healing of the nations. The current of spiritual life thrills the soul as the words of Christ are believed and practiced." [10]

The Church in Smyrna (Rev. 2:8-11) Situated on the eastern shore of the Aegean about 35 miles north of Ephesus, Smyrna had an excellent harbor and was second only to Ephesus in exports. Located at the end of the road crossing Phrygia and Lydia, Smyrna became a great trading city and rival of Ephesus.

While we have no information about the founding of the church at Smyrna, we have reason to believe that it was well organized by the turn of the century. Two features particularly arrest our attention as we read this letter: (1) Christ offers no rebuke, warning, or threat, and (2) the church is presently in the grip of severe persecution.

It is fitting, then, that the exalted Christ should come to this church with the introduction "The words of the first and the last, who died and came to life" (verse 8). Taken from the opening vision, the designation reassures the Christians facing arrest, trial, and possible death. The great need of the church is encouragement, not because the members are about to abandon Christ, but because of the barbaric cruelty and injustice of the persecution they face. During the centuries that were to follow, Christians in other places would become discouraged for significantly less reason and choose to abandon God's people.

We should note four things about the persecution in Smyrna (verses 9, 10): 1. John calls it *thlipsis*, tribulation or affliction, the idea being a crushing weight. The church at Smyrna felt trampled upon by the heavy heel of their wicked oppressors. Viewed symbolically, the Christians at Smyrna represent the universal church from about the close of the first century to the time when Constantine decided to tolerate all religions, including Christianity (A.D. 313). It was a period marked by intermittent persecution, and commentators have appropriately called it the Age of Martyrdom. [11]

No story of Christian martyrs during this time grips the imagination more than that of Polycarp, bishop of the church of Smyrna. Eusebius preserves the following account: "As Polycarp came into the arena a voice from heaven came to him: 'Be strong, Polycarp, and play the man.' . . . At length, when he stepped forward, he was asked by the proconsul if he really was Polycarp. When he said yes, the proconsul urged him to deny the charge. . . . The governor pressed him further: 'Swear and I will set you free: execrate Christ.' 'For eighty-six years,' replied Polycarp, 'I have been His servant, and He has never done me wrong: how can I blaspheme my King who saved me?' " [12]

2. The Christians suffered poverty. In the original Greek the word is *ptocheia*, denoting utter destitution. The church consisted mainly of converts from the poorer classes. But their meager state worsened as pagan mobs attacked without warning, breaking into their homes and plundering their goods. [13] Christ acknowledges their economic straits and then consoles them: "I know . . . your poverty (but you are rich)" (verse 9). This brings to mind words of the apostle James: "Has not God chosen those who are poor in the world to be rich in faith?" (James 2:5).

3. The Christians faced slander. The Jewish population in Smyrna directed outrageous accusations against the believers.

The Greek term is *blasphemia*. "The Martyrdom of Polycarp" mentions the Jewish hostility against the Christians: With "uncontrollable fury" the Jews and the heathen denounced Polycarp before the proconsul, and joined together in gathering wood and fagots to burn the Christian elder. [14] As in the case of the apostle Paul, Jewish wrath may have stemmed from Christian success in making converts of God fearers, Gentiles who were on the threshold of Judaism. [15]

John depicts the Jewish opponents as members of Satan's synagogue. In the Hebrew the word "Satan" means "accuser," "slanderer." The English word "synagogue" comes to us from the Greek and may be translated "gathering" or "congregation." While the slanderers call themselves Jews, they are in fact not Jews at all. Their malicious attacks against the church show that they belong, not to God's people, but actually to Satan's congregation. Jesus told some of the Jewish leaders of His day that their father was the devil, and not Abraham as they claimed, because by their opposition to Christ they unwittingly carried out Satan's will (see John 8:31-47). Paul stated that being a "real Jew" is not an external matter but an inward condition, since it is a matter of the heart (Rom. 2:28, 29).

Christians were charged with being cannibals, gathering for orgies, splitting up families, promoting atheism (because they didn't have images), being politically disloyal, and being incendiaries (because they predicted the world would end in flames). [16] In fact, so strong was the antagonism of some Jews toward the Christians that they would often stir up the pagans against the believers, as well as incite the Roman authorities in Smyrna against the Christians.

4. The Christians were imprisoned. John speaks of tribulation lasting for 10 days. He warns them of the impending suffering and assures them that it will be brief. In ancient times, prisons served only to hold the offender until the authorities decided what the actual punishment should be. For many Christians such confinement was "the prelude to death." [17] Thus the risen Lord holds out to them the promise and the reward for faithfulness: "I will give you the crown of life" (Rev. 2:10).

The word used for "crown" is *stephanos*, signifying the joy that comes from victory. The winners of the Olympic Games and of games that were held in the city of Smyrna received victors' crowns. A *stephanos* would also go to a city official for serving well throughout his term of office. And it was customary for pagans to wear such crowns at banquets and when they entered the temples of their gods for worship. Thus Christ offers the believers the *stephanos*, the crown of victory, for conquering the enemy in the spiritual battle of life, for their faithful service to Him. They would wear it at the great banquet at the end of time, and when they enter into the presence of God Himself.

The Church in Pergamum (Rev. 2:12-17) Pergamum was geographically situated on a tall, conical hill overlooking the valley of the Caicus River, the name of the city possibly meaning "citadel" in Greek (*Pergamon*). [18] While Ephesus and Smyrna achieved significance in the commercial world, Pergamum earned recognition in three areas: 1. It became a cultural center in Asia Minor. Its famous library of 200,000 parchment rolls was second only to the renowned library of Alexandria. According to one legend, the scholars of Pergamum invented parchment (made of animal hide) for writing when Ptolemy V of Egypt put an embargo on the export of papyrus to Alexandria's cultural rival.

2. Pergamum was an important religious center. On the upper terrace of the city the citizens erected their sacred and royal buildings, the most remarkable of which was the great altar of Zeus, protruding out near the top of the thousand-foot mountain. In addition to the worship of Zeus, three other cults flourished in Pergamum: Athena (the patron goddess), Dionysus, and Asclepios (the god of healing, commonly called "Saviour"). Galen, a famous physician in the ancient world, was a native of Pergamum who studied at the medical school of Asclepios.

3. Pergamum was the administrative center of Asia. Here the Roman proconsul set up his headquarters and made the city the official center for the imperial cult in Asia. By John's day Caesar worship had spread throughout the Roman Empire. As an act of political loyalty, everyone in the empire was required to appear before the local magistrates once a year, offer a pinch of incense before the bust of the emperor, and declare, "Caesar is Lord." Refusal meant persecution and death.

To the church in Pergamum, Christ comes as the one who has the "sharp two-edged sword" (verse 12). In the provincial capital the proconsul had the right of the sword, the power to execute at will. The designation thus serves to remind the Christians that the ultimate power over life and death belongs to God and not Rome.

Christ continues with an acknowledgment of the church's predicament: "I know where you dwell" (verse 13). It was not easy to be a Christian in Pergamum. Surrounded by paganism with its superstitious beliefs and immoral practices, the believers lived in a cultural climate hostile to their faith. Worse yet were the demands of emperor worship. At any moment the authorities could summon them before the proconsul and order them to pay homage to Caesar and denounce Christ. The presence of the imperial cult thus made Pergamum the place where Satan dwelt (verse 13), where he had set up his throne, where his rule was strongest. The reference to Antipas' martyrdom in Pergamum (verse 13) testifies to the satanical power of Rome. We have no information about Antipas except that he was faithful to the end. The title "faithful one" is the same as "faithful witness," used of Jesus (Rev. 1:5), indicating that Antipas was indeed a follower of the risen Lord. In the midst of such persecution, in the place where Satan had established his official seat, the church in Pergamum had remained loyal to Christ. The repeated emphasis on the city as the place where Satan dwells underlines the intensity of the conflict between God's people and the forces of evil.

In contrast to the courageous gallantry of the church as exemplified in the experience of Antipas, some in the church subscribed to "the teaching of Balaam" (Rev. 2:14) and to "the teaching of the Nicolaitans" (verse 15). John has called our attention to the latter in the letter to the Ephesian church.

From a study of Old Testament history we learn of Balaam's treason against God's people. For personal gain he advised the Midianite women on how to seduce the Israelites into sinning against the Lord, and thus bring about their defeat (see Num. 31:15, 16). Balaam, then, symbolizes the corrupt teachers in the Pergamum church who lured the believers into moral and religious compromise. The teaching of Balaam and of the Nicolaitans consisted of a lax stance toward pagan festivities. They encouraged fellow Christians to accommodate themselves to the religious and social requirements of pagan society. Through pagan food and pagan women Satan gained a foothold in the Pergamum church.

But the risen Lord does not take such compromise lightly. Christians are people called out from the world (Rev. 18:4, 5) to live to the glory of God (see Rev. 14:7). So Christ counsels the church to repent (Rev. 2:16). While only a portion of the membership lived treacherously, the church as a whole was guilty of irresponsible permissiveness. In contrast to the Ephesian church, which disciplined with loveless power, the Pergamum church failed to respond at all. Perhaps they rationalized their indifference as patient love, whereas in fact it proved to be a powerless policy.

Because of the seriousness of the Pergamum problem, Christ issues a threat: "I will come to you soon and war against them with the sword of my mouth" (verse 16). He is specifically concerned about those who adopted the policy of compromise in an effort to escape from the sword of Rome. Christ's sword is the sharp two-edged sword of His Word, which represents salvation to those who believe and obey, but judgment and condemnation to those who refuse it (see Heb. 4:12 and Eph. 6:17). Once again we encounter a climate of crisis that calls for a clear commitment to Christ. There is no room for compromise and no time to delay in taking one's stand! Jesus threatens, "I will come to you soon."

The message ends on a positive note (Rev. 2:17). To the faithful, Christ promises two things: 1. He will give them the hidden manna. The reference to hidden manna is rich with allusions to Israel's experience, the teaching of Jesus, and the worship of the church. First, we note the time in Israel's wilderness wanderings when they ran out of food and God provided them with manna (Ex. 16:11-15, 31). To preserve the memory of the event, Aaron, the high priest, put some manna in a jar and placed it in the ark before the Lord in the Most Holy Place of the sanctuary (verses 33, 34; Heb. 9:4). A psalm reciting Israel's history calls the manna "the grain of heaven" and "the bread of angels" (Ps. 78:24, 25).

Second, in His discourse to the multitude the day after the miraculous meal, Jesus refers to Himself as the "bread of life," the "bread which came down from heaven" (John 6:48, 51). Those who eat such bread will "live for ever" (verse 51). The bread that Christ refers to is His body, which He sacrificed for us all.

Finally, the church preserves the memory of Christ's life and teaching and proclaims the saving significance of His sacrifice when it celebrates the Lord's Supper (1 Cor. 11:23-26). In contrast to the food offered in sacrifice to pagan gods and served in temple festivities, the early Christians partook of the bread of heaven in anticipation of that day when they would sit at table with the risen Lord in His glorious kingdom. But to enjoy the blessings of heaven in the future, they must in the present refuse to share in the earthly benefits of spiritual compromise.

2. He will give them a white stone and a new name.[19] In John's day the white stone would bring to mind the common custom of issuing a *tessera*, a small tablet of wood, metal, or stone, as a token of recognition to winners at the Olympic Games, to gladiators who over the years had won the admiration of the crowds, or to officials for faithful service. The reference to the new name[20] reflects an Old Testament custom of granting a new status to the recipient. In connection with the covenant transaction, God changed the name of Abram to Abraham to signify his new role as father of many nations (Gen. 17:5), and in the case of Jacob, He changed the patriarch's name to Israel to indicate the new relationship he would enjoy as a result of the divine blessing (Gen. 32:28, 29). For the Pergamum believers the white stone and new name represent the recognition and glorious status to be awarded them in the new earth for their loyal service to Christ and moral triumph over the enemy.

The Church in Thyatira (Rev. 2:18-29)   Thyatira was the weakest, the least famous, and the most obscure of the seven cities of Revelation. The paucity of information about it increases the challenge of understanding the church's actual situation. Ironically, the fate of the city reflects that of the church. Ramsay shares this view of Thyatira: "It is one of those cities whose situation exposes them to destruction by every conqueror, and yet compels their restoration after every siege and sack. It lies right in the track of invasion; it blocks the way and must be captured by an invader; it guards the passage to a rich district, and hence the barbarity of the assailant: but it could never be made a really strong fortress in ancient warfare, so as to resist successfully."[21]

The church in Thyatira quite appropriately represents that period in church history commonly called the Dark Ages. During those centuries church tradition replaced the Bible as the basis of instruction, a human priesthood overshadowed the priesthood of Jesus, and for those who resisted the corrupting influences of the established organization, persecution became the order of the day.[22]

Thyatira's letter begins with a threatening description of the exalted Christ: "The words of the Son of God, who has eyes like a flame of fire, and whose feet are like burnished bronze" (verse 18). In the introductory vision Jesus appears as "a son of man" (Rev. 1:13), but here the title shifts to Son of God. The designation refutes the imperial cult claim that the emperor was as a god, and issues a warning against those in the church who had become lax on this point.

The flaming eyes and feet of burnished bronze represent the penetrating power of Christ's gaze and the uncompromising stance toward the corrupting influences in the church. With careful scrutiny He examines the inner sanctum of the human heart, bringing to light both good and evil in the church.

But first He acknowledges those who have refused to compromise: "I know your works, your love and faith and service and patient endurance, and that your latter works exceed the first" (Rev. 2:19). The service that Christ commends has love as its motivation, and the patient endurance He approves is the fruit of faith. In contrast to the Christians in Ephesus who regressed in their spiritual life, at least some of the believers in Thyatira have grown, and they have achieved it under the most unfavorable circumstances. Their experience proves that spiritual maturation can take place even in churches darkened by moral compromise and deprivation. No one can excuse their own moral failure by blaming someone else. Christian service and steadfastness are the fruit of love and faith, gifts of the Spirit available to all believers.

Such good works stand in bold contrast to the evil deeds of the faithless. And yet Christ rebukes the church for tolerating the woman Jezebel. Attempts to identify the woman (or what the image represents if it is a symbol rather than an actual person) have been of little help, except to make clear that the real threat to the church came from within its ranks. From the letter we learn four things (verses 20, 21):

1. She was a wicked woman. The name Jezebel conjures up images of immoral conduct and base religious practices. Whoever she was, she resembled the Phoenician princess who married Ahab, the Israelite king, and subsequently brought into the northern kingdom the worship of Baal with its gross licentiousness.

2. She claimed to be a prophetess. In the letter to the Ephesians, Jesus through John commended the church for recognizing false apostles (verse 2); and in the message to the church in Smyrna, He referred to false Jews (verse 9). Here He calls attention to the false prophetess. We must understand her claim to the prophetic office, not in the sense of one who sees into the future and utters predictions, but in the sense of one who claims to speak for God or as one having insight into the

truth. The person or persons portrayed as Jezebel sought to lead the church in a new and destructive direction.

3. She lured church members into immorality and idolatry. The Bible often refers to idolatry as religious adultery. Scripture brands Israel's infidelity as harlotry (Ex. 34:15, 16; Deut. 31:16; Hosea 9:1; Jer. 2:20-28; Eze. 23:1-3). But the evidence suggests that licentiousness as well as idol worship plagued the church at Thyatira. Barclay understands the phrase "the deep things of Satan" (Rev. 2:24) to be a reference to sexual sins: "Some of them [the heretics] held that it was a plain duty to experience every kind of sin. The real achievement was to allow the body to wallow in sin and to keep the soul unaffected. Those who knew the deep things of Satan were those who had deliberately plumbed evil to its depths." [23]

Apparently the teaching and seduction of the self-styled prophetess was a type of spiritual infidelity that resulted in physical intimacy. The city of Thyatira was known for its rich variety of trades and the guilds of the craftsmen employed in them. It was customary for the workers to share a common meal that they often ate in a temple, and which they began and ended in a ritual of sacrifice to the gods. Moreover, it was not uncommon for such communal meals to involve drinking and carousing. Those who chose not to attend the meals or participate in the rituals risked economic sanctions comparable in many respects to those who decline to join trade unions today.

Apparently the woman Jezebel led a strong movement in the church that sought to promote the trade guilds and the activities associated with them in the interests of business and commercial prosperity, and attempted to justify her position with theological rationale. Thyatira's Jezebel proceeded not from principle but from a desire for personal gain.

4. She refused to repent. While the risen Lord is merciful, He will not take lightly the deeds of one who finds in His mercy an opportunity to advance his wicked cause. "I gave her time to repent, but she refuses to repent of her immorality" (verse 21). The penetrating gaze of Christ's flaming eyes exposes the woman's motivation.

Threats and promises follow: "I will throw her on a sickbed, and those who commit adultery with her I will throw into great tribulation, unless they repent of her doings; and I will strike her children dead. And all the churches shall know that I am he who searches mind and heart, and I will give to each of you as your works deserve" (verses 22, 23). The time for Jezebel's repentance has passed. Her judgment is imminent, and the announcement of her punishment seeks to awaken those lured by her into sin and to lead them to repent.

Unlike the fate of the Old Testament Jezebel, [24] the false prophetess' punishment comes in the form of an illness that leaves her bedridden. Her condition will serve as a reminder to the church that willful sin ends in ruin. She made her bed, and now she is compelled to lie in it. As to the punishment of her followers, it appears more severe. Perhaps that is because Christ gives them more warning and thus expects them to benefit from the punishment they see meted out to her.

To those who have remained loyal to Him, Christ offers a twofold promise (verses 26-28): First is the offer of power over the nations—actually a reference to Psalm 2:8, 9, which depicts the time when the conquering Messiah will break the back of pagan aggression and resistance and extend the rule of Israel to the ends of the earth. When applied to Christ, these Psalm 2 verses point to the ultimate victory over evil that ushers in the kingdom at the last day (Rev. 20:4; 22:5). Here the Revelation 2 text describes the reward of the faithful in the church at Thyatira. They will reign with the risen Lord.

Christ promises them also the morning star. At the end of the book of Revelation, Jesus calls Himself "the bright morning star" (Rev. 22:16). The believers will not only reign with Christ but will be forever with Him. Here is the promise of life eternal: "He who has the Son has life" (1 John 5:12).

---

[1] R. C. Trench, in Barclay, *The Revelation of John*, verse 1, p. 60.

[2] Jack Finegan, *The Archeology of the New Testament*, p. 164.

[3] *Ibid.*, p. 165.

[4] See Ramsay, *The Letters to the Seven Churches*, pp. 210-236.

[5] Barclay attributes this designation to Ignatius (Barclay, p. 58), who served as a bishop in Antioch during the latter part of the first century.

[6] In the Ephesus Museum one may see a marble statue of Artemis, dating back to the reign of Domitian (A.D. 81-96). She appears short, dark, and multibreasted, indicating that she was a goddess of fertility.

[7] E. K. Simpson, "Commentary on the Epistle to the Ephesians," in *The New International Commentary on the New Testament: Commentary on the Epistles to the Ephesians and the Colossians*, p. 17.

[8] *The SDA Bible Commentary*, Ellen G. White Comments, vol. 7, p. 956.

[9] Ramsay, pp. 248, 249.

[10] *The SDA Bible Commentary*, Ellen G. White Comments, vol. 7, p. 957.

[11] *The SDA Bible Commentary*, vol. 7, p. 746.

[12] Eusebius *Ecclesiastical History*, 4. 15. 17-20.

[13] See Barclay, p. 79.

[14] *The Ante-Nicene Fathers*, vol. 1, pp. 41, 42.

[15] Mounce, in *The Book of Revelation*, pp. 92, 93.

[16] Barclay, pp. 80, 81.

[17] *Ibid.*, p. 79.

[18] Ramsay believes the name was derived from the preparation of parchment (*pergamēne*) for writing purposes (Ramsay, p. 290).

[19] See Barclay, pp. 95-97.

[20] A new name represents a change in character (*The SDA Bible Commentary*), vol. 7, p. 750.

[21] Ramsay, p. 323.

[22] *The SDA Bible Commentary*, vol. 7, p. 750.

[23] Barclay, p. 109.

[24] 2 Kings 9:30-37 presents Jezebel's death in lurid detail. Two or three eunuchs threw her to her death from an upper story window, and before her remains were recovered, dogs had consumed most of them. Her violent death was consistent with the way she had lived.

Messages to the
Seven Churches—II

(Based on Revelation 3)

"Let your light so shine before men, that they may see your good works and give glory to your Father who is in heaven" (Matt. 5:16).

The Church in Sardis (Rev. 3:1-6)   The history of the rise and decline of the city of Sardis provides an excellent background against which to read and interpret Revelation's letter to the church. William Ramsay sees in the form of the letter a reflection of the ancient history of the city. [1] We first hear of Sardis in the seventh century B.C., when it flourished as the capital of the Lydian kingdom. It became one of the greatest cities in the ancient world, but by John's time it had lost its vitality and was trying to live on the prestige of its past.

Situated on a 1,500-foot-high spur of Mount Tmolus, the original city appeared like an impregnable fortress overlooking the fertile fields of the Hermus Valley. Because of its situation on a narrow plateau and because of the steep and difficult approach to it, the inhabitants of the city could easily defend it against invading armies. Such features contributed to the Sardians complacency toward their city's security. Capitalizing on this attitude, some Persian troops one night made their way up the precipitous ridge by a fault in the rock, found the city unguarded, and took it by surprise. [2]

Following the Persian conquest, Sardis disappeared from history for 200 years. We hear of it next when it fell to Alexander the Great, and then to Antiochus the Great. Some of his soldiers climbed the steep cliffs by night as the Persians had done centuries before, and thus the city was captured once again. In 190 B.C. the kingdom of Pergamum incorporated the city, and then Sardis became part of the Roman province of Asia when Pergamum fell to Rome.

An affluent city, with part of its wealth said to have come from gold found in the Pactolus River, Sardis was strategically located on an important highway connecting the Persian city of Susa to prominent cities in Asia Minor. Sardis derived income from the manufacture of woolen goods. In addition, the city was the first in history to mint gold and silver coins, and may have been the first to discover the art of dyeing wool.

Sardis continued to enjoy prosperity during the Roman period, despite a devastating earthquake in A.D. 17. The city's reconstruction resulted from the generosity of the emperor Tiberius, who donated the equivalent of $1 million to have it rebuilt and remitted the city's taxes for five years.

When John wrote the book of Revelation, Sardis was still a city of wealth, but its affluence was deceptive because it resulted from its fortuitous location and help from Rome rather than from the diligence and industry of its residents. Living in such an atmosphere, the Christians had apparently absorbed the city's character. They became listless and lethargic, earning the reputation of being alive when in fact they were spiritually dead (Rev. 3:1).

The risen Lord approaches the church in Sardis as one "who has the seven spirits of God and the seven stars" (verse 1). The description conveys two basic truths: 1. The universal presence and active ministry of the Holy Spirit. The lifeless believers in Sardis need to have the power of the Holy Spirit revitalize them. Paul's counsel to the Christians in Rome also applies to the church in Sardis: "If the Spirit of him who raised Jesus from the dead dwells in you, he . . . will give life to your mortal bodies" (Rom. 8:11). Sardis is a church of past splendor and steady decline. But what interests the Lord is their present character, not their past reputation.

2. The close relationship between Christ and the church. In the introductory vision of the exalted Christ, John saw Him holding the seven stars in His right hand (Rev. 1:16). This vision identifies the seven stars as the angels to the seven churches (verse 20). The picture of Christ cupping them in His hand signifies not only His tender regard for the church but also the truth that the church belongs to Him. The hands nailed to the wood of the cross also bear the church, which He purchased with His blood.

Christ knows His church. The Christians at Sardis, for the most part, have fallen into spiritual complacency through adaptation and compromise to their pagan environment. Jesus finds much to condemn about them, and little to commend. Of the

seven, the church at Sardis receives the most severe denuncia-
tion from the risen Lord. His counsel consists of five commands
(Rev. 3:2, 3):

1. He tells them to awake. The exhortation to watch takes on
added significance in light of the city's military history. The
church must maintain a posture of constant vigilance in view of
the impending crisis facing God's people. Throughout the New
Testament we find admonitions and warnings to watch and be
ready (for example, Mark 13:33-37), to "keep awake and be sober"
(1 Thess. 5:6). The church lives in a climate of conflict and must
maintain a militant position if it is to triumph.

2. He enjoins them to "strengthen what remains." The
Sardian Christians have reached the point of spiritual death, but
restoration is still possible. The church is to rebuild by reinforc-
ing itself with the positive truths of the gospel. Christ's complaint
is that their works are not perfect. Sardis fails to measure up to
God's expectations, to accomplish fully what He calls them to do.

From the top of the acropolis on which the ancient city of
Sardis stood, the Christians could see the unfinished temple of
the Greek god Artemis, worked on in three phases from around
300 B.C. to around A.D. 150.[3] It was dedicated to Cybele, a local
goddess who, according to pagan belief, had the power to restore
the dead to life. The Christians at Sardis were like that unfinished
temple. Before God their works were incomplete. Ellen White
understands the condition in the Sardis church to be, in part, the
result of petty quarrels over minor points of doctrine, and makes
a homiletic application: "There are many ready to die spiritually,
and the Lord calls upon us to strengthen them. God's people are
to be firmly united in the bonds of Christian fellowship, and are
to be strengthened in the faith by speaking often to one another
about the precious truths entrusted to them. Never are they to
spend their time in accusing and condemning one another."[4]

Viewed symbolically, the Sardis church represents the period
of violent doctrinal controversy among the newly established
Protestant churches. It was a time when doctrinal study gave
way to the development of creeds, and rationalism and scientific
discovery produced an apathy toward spiritual pursuits. The
rigid formulas of Protestant orthodoxy contributed to the spiritual decline of the members, many who became Christians in
name only, having a form of godliness but lacking spiritual
vitality.[5]

3. Christ instructs them to remember what they received and

heard. The form of the verb *remember* indicates a continuous action. The believers are to refresh their memory of the truths of the gospel constantly, because they face the temptations of the enemy daily. Concerning the Lord's Supper, the apostle Paul wrote, "I received from the Lord what I also delivered to you" (1 Cor. 11:23). Christians are to observe the Communion service "in remembrance" of Christ (verse 24). Remembering is more than recalling the past. It is the means by which we relive the past and preserve its significance for the present. Forgetting, then, is spiritually lethal. Twice in Sardis' history its acropolis had fallen to the enemy because the defenders had failed to remember their past history.

4. He admonishes them to hold on to what they are remembering. Christians must preserve the faith by taking active measures against the corrupting influences of their pagan surroundings. They must maintain a watchful eye, guarding the treasure of truths entrusted to them. The picture of the church is that of a watchtower in the ancient city of Sardis, with its members serving as sentinels. Barclay has put it well: " 'Eternal vigilance is the price of liberty' and eternal watchfulness is the price of salvation." [6]

5. Christ summons them to repent. In view of the imminent end, the call to repentance is urgent. The condition of the church at Sardis is serious, and they have no time to delay. They are "on the point of death" (Rev. 3:2) because the course they are pursuing is destructive to their faith. Christ attempts to arrest their attention and redirect their steps before it is too late.

A sober threat follows His urgent call to repent. If the church fails to heed the warning, Christ will visit them unexpectedly with judgment. The expression "I will come like a thief " (verse 3) reminds the reader of Jesus' discourse to His disciples about His coming (Matt. 24:42-44, 48-51), and the counsel of the apostles (see 1 Thess. 5:2; 2 Peter 3:10). But the divine visitation in the message to the Sardian church is not the second advent of Jesus, but a judgment that will take place prior to that event. [7] Sardis' perilous position stems from their failure to watch. Their unguarded condition leaves them vulnerable to the enemy. Here is a paradox. If the Christians fail to keep watch, the risen Lord will take them by surprise and mete out judgment. While He is not the enemy of the church, their refusal to repent makes them enemies of Jesus. [8]

Although the future of the church looks grim, there does still exist a small minority of believers, "a few names in Sardis" (Rev. 3:4), whose faith has remained pure. They do not soil their garments (verse 4) by adapting themselves to the contaminating pagan culture. The religious life that God approves of consists of moral action and ethical behavior arising from faith in Jesus. A purity of inner motive produces an outer cleanness.

The faithful in Sardis will "walk" with the exalted Christ "in white" (verse 4). One commentator sees the expression as alluding to early Christian baptism, the believer being clothed in white robes after he emerged from the water, to symbolize the cleansing of his life. [9] Elsewhere in the book of Revelation we find a reference to the redeemed who have "washed their robes and made them white" (Rev. 7:14; cf. Rev. 22:14) through faith in Jesus' atoning sacrifice. The scene is one of triumph (Rev. 7:9, 10) through tribulation. To walk with the risen Lord in white, then, means to take positive steps to guard against the corrupting influences of the world, and to move forward in faith through dynamic Christian living.

The message to the church in Sardis ends with a threefold promise (Rev. 3:4): 1. The faithful will receive white garments. The garments represent the transformed character, as manifested in righteous deeds made possible through faith in Jesus. The garments are emblems of a moral conquest and spiritual triumph over the evil forces in the world. [10]

2. Christ will not blot their names out of the book of life. The picture points back to Moses' intercessory prayer on behalf of his people (Ex. 32:32, 33), and reflects an Old Testament custom of registering the names of all those who held citizenship in the community of Israel (see Eze. 13:9; Ezra 2:62). At the end-time only those who have their names written in the book of life (Dan. 12:1; Rev. 21:27) will receive deliverance from tribulation, while the wicked end up in the lake of fire (Rev. 20:15).

3. Christ will confess their names before His Father and the angels. Here the vision emphasizes the reward for faithfulness. Those who have acknowledged Christ in the face of trial, He will in turn acknowledge in God's presence (Matt. 10:32; read verses 24-33). We find Jesus making a close correlation between the positive way we respond under the pressure of tribulation and the reward we will receive in the hour of triumph.

The Church in Philadelphia (Rev. 3:7-13)   Colonists from Pergamum founded the youngest city of the seven churches of Revelation on the edge of a volcanic plain. They established it during the second century before Christ for the expressed purpose of spreading Greek culture and language through the central regions of Asia. The city's strategic location on the imperial post route from Rome by way of Troas made it a "gateway to the East" (the "open door" in verse 8). Being on the main line of imperial communication thus made it a center of commerce, as well as Greek culture.

The lava and ashes of extinct volcanoes rendered the land near and around the city of Philadelphia most fertile. In time the city became the center of a grape-growing and famous winery industry. But its geographical location left it subject to frequent tremors and occasional major earthquakes. The earthquake in A.D. 17 that devastated Sardis also brought considerable damage to Philadelphia. As in the case with Sardis, Tiberius contributed toward the rebuilding of the city, and in gratitude the city changed its name to Neo-Caesarea (the New Caesarea, or the New City of Caesar). Nero restored the name Philadelphia to the city. The city, however, altered it on two other occasions to honor Rome. [11]

Philadelphia receives praise and encouragement but no rebuke from the Lord. Three descriptions of Christ introduce Him to this church (verse 7): 1. He is the holy one. More than any other expression, "the holy one" describes the divine essence, or innermost nature, of the Deity. [12] The expression is a frequent title in the book of Isaiah (for example, Isa. 1:4; 5:19, 24; 10:17, 20; 40:25; 41:14, 16, 20; 43:3, 14, 15), but appears less often in the New Testament. The description of Jesus as the holy one is rare, and John uses it to emphasize Christ's deity. As the holy one, Jesus shares the very nature, the divine essence, of God.

2. He is the true one. We must view the expression in the context of verse 9, which refers to "those of the synagogue of Satan" who call themselves Jews "and are not, but lie." Their rejection of Christ proves that they are not real Jews. The allusion reminds us of Christ's debate with certain unbelieving Jews who claimed to be descendants of Abraham and thus children of God. Jesus refuted their unbelieving arrogance and declared them to be of the devil, the father of lies (John 8:33-44). The "true one" stresses Christ's reality or authenticity. In contrast to the false Jews, Jesus is the true Messiah. His genuineness exposes the counterfeit or unreal nature of such people.

3. He has the key of David. The phrase "key of David" alludes to the messianic passage of Isaiah 22:22: "I will place on his

shoulder the key of the house of David; he shall open, and none shall shut; and he shall shut, and none shall open." The context makes clear that the key symbolizes the authority granted to Eliakim (verses 20, 21), the servant of King Hezekiah. As a designation of the exalted Christ, the expression ascribes to Jesus the supreme or undisputed authority over who will enter the Holy City. John may here be attempting to encourage those Christians excommunicated from the local synagogue because of their loyalty to Jesus. [13]

The Messianic ascription leads to a series of three promises (Rev. 3:8-10): 1. Christ has set before the church "an open door" that no one can shut. It is possible to understand the expression as a prediction of the church's missionary activity under the lordship of the risen Christ. Viewed this way, the prophetic statement offers hope to those whose witness appears hampered by opposition from the Jewish population. As the city centuries earlier disseminated the language and culture of the Greeks, so the church would spread throughout the regions of Asia the gospel of the risen Christ. [14]

We may also see the "open door" as an encouragement to those Christians in Philadelphia shut out from the local synagogue. In this case the expression would serve to remind the believers that Christ has opened the way to the kingdom. While their Jewish opponents may keep them out of the synagogue, they cannot prevent them from entering the kingdom of heaven. The local meeting place that excludes them has become the "synagogue of Satan," and so they cannot expect to find spiritual nurture there. But Jesus has opened a new and better way to God, and no one will be able to hinder the believers from going directly to the Father through faith in the risen Lord (see John 10:7, 9).

It seems reasonable, then, to interpret the "open door" as unlimited access to the measureless resources of God's grace: "Those who are seeking to be faithful to God may be denied many of the privileges of the world; their way may be hedged up and their work hindered by the enemies of truth; but there is no power that can close the door of communication between God and their souls." [15] The "open door" places those who have "little power" (Rev. 3:8) in a position to receive divine strength that will sustain them in their hour of trial.

2. Christ will bring the hostile Jews to submission. Here we move to the heart of the conflict between the church and the

synagogue in Philadelphia. From the similarity of the messages to the churches in Smyrna and Philadelphia, we may conclude that the conditions within and without both churches were much the same. Of the seven churches, they are the only ones that receive unqualified praise. They appear impoverished (Smyrna) and impotent (Philadelphia) but are really wealthy and strong in faith. The Christians in both churches face persecution from the local Jewish leaders, whose claim to be the people of God the Lord now refutes. The messages to both churches say that such Jews actually belong to the synagogue of Satan. For by their malicious treatment of the church, they betray their true origin and unholy calling.

In Christ's words of assurance to the Philadelphian believers, we find echoed Jewish eschatological expectation. In Old Testament prophetic literature and especially in the book of Isaiah we find expressed the belief that in the new age about to dawn, the nations of the world will pay humble homage to the Jews, bowing down at their feet in submission (Isa. 45:14; 49:23; 60:14; Zech. 8:22, 23). A severe rebuke to the Jews, the words of the risen Lord testify to the fact that the church and not the synagogue will now be the sphere of God's redemptive grace in Christ. The church replaces the Jewish nation as the true heir of the divine promises. Unbelieving Jews will recognize Christ's love for His church (Rev. 3:9) when they witness the triumph of His people.

3. Christ will keep His followers from the hour of trial. Some see in the promise an allusion to the pretribulation rapture of the church. But the context does not support this view, nor does the thrust of the verse (verse 10) itself. [16] The "hour of trial" from which God shelters the believers "is coming on the whole world" for the purpose of trying "those who dwell upon the earth." The latter phrase occurs eight more times in the book of Revelation (Rev. 6:10; 8:13; 11:10 [twice]; 13:8, 14; 14:6; 17:8), and in each of these verses it refers to the wicked. [17] The hour of trial spoken of in Revelation 3:10 thus refers to God's judgment meted out to the enemies of His people prior to the Second Advent. Through their patient endurance the Christians have kept the faith, and here Christ assures them that He will keep them from the wrath of God's judgment (cf. Rev. 14:6-12).

The keynote of the book of Revelation follows next: "I am coming soon" (Rev. 3:11). The reference to Christ's return here appears in striking contrast to the threatening ones in the message to Ephesus (He will come and remove their lampstand

[Rev. 2:5]), to Pergamum (He will come and make war against them with the sword of His mouth [verse 16]), and to Sardis (He will come as a thief and take them by surprise [Rev. 3:3]). Christ's coming to the church in Philadelphia occurs at the time of the Second Advent (see Rev. 22:20). In view of His soon return, Christ exhorts the faithful to hold fast what they have and to surrender their crowns to no one (see Rev. 3:11). Instead of being a threat to the church, Christ's words offer encouragement to endure in light of the fact that the end is near. The conclusion of their tribulation will be the beginning of their triumph.

The crown Christ promises the believers is like the winner's wreath awarded in an athletic conquest (see 1 Cor. 9:24-27; 2 Tim. 4:6-8). But unlike the Olympic race, Christ grants the reward not only to the one who finishes first but to everyone who completes the race. The emphasis is on endurance to the end.

The exalted Christ concludes with two additional promises (Rev. 3:12): 1. Those who overcome receive the promise of permanent residence with God. Christ will make them pillars in God's temple. Christ's message may have had several things in mind here: a. The picture of a fixed pillar in the temple of God would be consoling to Christians expelled from the synagogue, and thus displaced in the community. b. The recurring earthquakes that terrorized the citizens of Philadelphia and forced them to evacuate to the open country was an experience well known to the church. The many temples in the city failed to provide a safe refuge during such tremors, thus leaving the people to shift for themselves. In such an atmosphere of uncertainty and instability, the believers would find in Christ's words the promise of security and lasting peace. They will never go out of God's temple. c. In the architecture of ancient temples, pillars served both a practical function and an aesthetic one. They provided support to the massive superstructure, and gave the buildings a majesty and magnificence that inspired awe. Christ is telling His followers that He will honor them with dignity and splendor before His Father because of their loyalty to Him despite the personal humiliation and public disgrace they received from their persecutors.

2. To His faithful followers Christ offers the threefold promise of a new name: a. On them He will write the name of His Father, signifying new *ownership*. He calls the believers by God's name because they now belong to Him. b. On them Christ will place the name of God's City, the New Jerusalem, signifying new

citizenship. c. And on them Christ will inscribe His own new name, signifying a new *partnership*. Through their steadfast love and patient endurance, the Christians participated in Christ's sufferings, and now the risen Lord invites them to share in His glory.

Earlier the apostle Paul had written to the Philippians about God exalting Jesus to a position of preeminence, bestowing "on him the name which is above every name, that at the name of Jesus every knee should bow" (Phil. 2:9, 10). And in his letter to the Ephesians, he tells us that God has raised us up with Christ, and made us "sit with him in the heavenly places in Christ Jesus" (Eph. 2:6). Here in the message to Philadelphia the risen Lord tells us that we will share the grandeur and glory of His great triumph by bearing His name. It is an honor that lasts throughout eternity.[18]

The Church in Laodicea (Rev. 3:14-22)   William Barclay refers to Laodicea as having "the grim distinction of being the only church of which the risen Christ has nothing good to say."[19] Its condemnation is absolute and total. The Lord cannot find even a faithful remnant as He had discovered in Sardis, the church at the point of death.

Because of its position on the Roman road from Ephesus to the east and to Syria, the city of Laodicea became one of the great commercial and financial centers of the ancient world. Three facts about the city help us understand the letter to the church: 1. Laodicea enjoyed a prosperous agricultural economy. Situated in the fertile Lycus Valley, the city had access to good grazing ground for its sheep, and in time developed through careful breeding black wool of high quality. As a result, a clothing manufacturing industry flourished to such an extent that the city became famous throughout the ancient world for its various garments. Christ's description of the church as naked would thus be a stinging rebuke to those living in a city that took pride in the quality of its clothes. And His counsel to buy from Him white garments would constitute a blow to the smugness associated with the wealth derived from the famous black wool.

2. Laodicea became a hub of the banking industry. The prosperity from its agriculture and commerce made Laodicea an extremely wealthy city. The Roman statesman Cicero wrote of cashing his treasury bills there.[20] And we read of large quantities of gold stored in the city.[21] An indication of Laodicea's wealth also comes to us from the Roman historian Tacitus. Writing of

the city's destruction by an earthquake in A.D. 60, he notes, "One of the most famous cities of Asia, Laodicea, was in that same year overthrown by an earthquake and without any relief from us recovered itself by its own resources."[22] When an earthquake had devastated Sardis, the citizens had built a temple in gratitude to Rome for its assistance in reconstructing the city, and Philadelphia had changed its name in appreciation for similar help. But the rich and independent Laodicea proudly refused imperial subsidies, and drew from its own reserves instead. Apparently such pride and independence found expression in the attitude of the church, and provoked the complaint and counsel of the risen Christ (Rev. 3:17, 18).

3. Laodicea established a prominent medical center. The medical school, at first connected with the nearby temple of an ancient Carian god (named Men) believed to have healing powers, later moved to the city. The Laodicean medical school achieved its reputation from its own pharmaceutical preparations. Following the teachings of Herophilus (c.330-c.250 B.C.), who advocated the view that compound diseases could be treated best by compound medicines, the physicians developed a number of products, including an ointment for ears and a salve for eyes. Composed of "Phrygian powder mixed with oil," the eyesalve became a common medication for treating eye diseases. In time other medical schools recognized its healing properties and imported the Phrygian stone from which the Laodicean physicians made the powder. The reputation of the medical school at Laodicea thus brought recognition to the city as a center for the treatment of eye diseases.[23] To the church in a city that took pride in its medical facilities and that boasted of its famous eyesalve, Christ comes with condemnation and counsel: They are blind and need His healing grace.

The apostle Paul refers to the church in Laodicea four times in his letter to the Colossians. He speaks of striving "for those at Laodicea, and for all who have not seen my face" (Col. 2:1). The latter phrase has led to speculation that the Laodicean church contained people who were blind or were suffering from poor eye sight.[24] In the conclusion of his letter, Paul instructs the Colossians to exchange letters with the Christians in Laodicea, and to exhort Archippus, possibly the pastor of the Laodicean church, to "fulfil the ministry which you have received in the Lord" (Col. 4:16, 17). Paul's letter to the Laodiceans has vanished. Barclay interprets the apostle's counsel as a stern reproof to the resident minister (Archippus), and suggests that as early as 30 years before the writing of the book of Revelation, "rot had set in the church in Laodicea and an unsatisfactory ministry had sown the seeds of degeneration."[25] If so, it would make the later condition of the church all the more serious and the message of Christ all the more urgent.

The message to the church in Laodicea begins with a series of three descriptions of the risen Lord (Rev. 3:14): 1. He is the Amen. The word comes to us from the Hebrew and means "trustworthy." To a Hebrew-speaking church this would be clear, but the Laodicean congregation spoke and read Greek. The words "faithful and true witness," which follow, help clarify the meaning. In the Hebrew text of Isaiah 65:16, we find the expression "God of Amen" (rendered in English as "God of truth"), where *Amen* serves to stress the reliability of the words of those who bless themselves or take an oath by God's name. As a designation of Christ, it affirms the validity and binding quality of His testimony.

2. He is the faithful and true witness. Here the vision further emphasizes the trustworthiness of Christ's message. The added stress sharpens the focus on the faithlessness of the Laodicean church. As the faithful and true witness of God, Jesus bears testimony that exposes the true condition of the church and discloses the impending judgment should the church fail to heed Christ's counsel.

3. He is the beginning of God's creation. We must understand such a designation against the background of two other New Testament passages: a. Paul uses a similar expression in his letter to the Colossians when he describes the work of Christ (Col. 1:15-20). The fact that the cities of Laodicea and Colossae were in close proximity to each other, and that Paul instructs the Colossians to exchange letters with the Laodiceans, suggests that in all probability the reader would understand the description of Jesus as the "beginning of God's creation" in the Pauline sense. In both letters the designation refers to Christ's mediatory role in the creation of the world. b. The fourth Gospel provides the clearest and most elaborate statement attesting to Christ's work as Creator, and, at the same time, declares His eternal nature (John 1:1-3). Revelation's ascription to Christ is consistent with the teaching of the fourth Gospel and asserts that the One who bears testimony is the One who began the process of creation. All things originate with Him.

Words of condemnation follow next (Rev. 3:15-17): 1. The Laodiceans are lukewarm. The expression takes on a new significance when we remember the hot mineral-laden springs of Hierapolis, a city six miles to the north of Laodicea, and the pure, cold waters of Colossae, about 11 miles to the south and east. The famous hot water of Hierapolis flowed out from the city across a wide plateau, eventually spilling over a cliff 300 feet high and a mile wide. The plumes of steam from the hot water cascading over the rocky edge formed a spectacular sight that the Laodiceans could enjoy from a distance. Such hot waters served a medicinal purpose for those with tired muscles and aching bones. [26] Since Laodicea had an insufficient natural water supply, the city depended on water piped from hot springs to the south of the city. By the time it reached Laodicea, however, the water was tepid and nauseous, providing neither refreshment for the weary nor healing for the sick.

The church's basic problem is its lukewarm condition. Their pride, self-sufficiency, and virtual ignorance make them indifferent to their perilous position with the risen Lord. They lack a zest for spiritual living and the motivation to do something about it. And their indifference is so distasteful to Christ that He speaks of vomiting.

2. The Laodiceans are wretched, pitiable, poor, blind, and naked. Nowhere else do we find such a deplorable description. The city's Christians exist in a state of wretchedness. The word translated in the English as "wretched" is the same one Paul uses to describe the condition of one in bondage to sin (Rom. 7:24). It appears in James' description of the rich who "weep and howl" (James 5:1) in the last days because of the judgment facing them for their exploiting the poor. One should *pity* the Christians at Laodicea. They live in spiritual misery and remain completely oblivious to their condition. Their affliction does not evoke compassion but disgust, since it is the result of their self-centered and self-absorbed ways.

The Laodiceans are *poor*, *blind*, and *naked*, three words that exemplify their wretchedness and show why they, of all the churches, should be pitied. In the original Greek the word translated "poor" denotes a beggarly existence brought about by abject poverty. As a witness to the truth in Jesus, a light to a world in darkness, the Christians of Laodicea are worthless. They are spiritually impoverished. And it resulted from their rejection of the resources of God's grace, just as their city had spurned financial help from Rome following its destruction by the earthquake in A.D. 60.

The blindness of the Laodiceans becomes evident in their conceit and ignorance as reflected in their self-praise: "I am rich, I have prospered, and I need nothing" (Rev. 3:17). Jesus says the opposite is true. We naturally wonder how it is that they could be so far from the truth. Their blindness has a twofold aspect: they claim not only to be spiritually rich but also to have achieved their wealth on their own.

Most embarrassing of all, the Laodicean Christians are shamefully naked—and ignorant of that fact. Laodicea prides itself on its financial wealth, famous eyesalve, and textile industry, and could appeal to its banking establishment, medical school, and manufacturing center in support of its claims of greatness. The risen Lord thus strikes at the core of the Laodicean problem: the very things that have brought them material success have also placed them at the brink of spiritual ruin. They stand in need of everything! Buying three essentials will turn their condition around (Rev. 3:18):

1. Christ counsels them to buy from Him "gold refined by fire." The expression points to the Laodiceans' need to place their confidence in God's Word and the testimony of Jesus, and not in the things that the world has to offer. The gold that the church needs is the faith made pure in the heat of persecution. The fiery trials purge the believers of the entanglements of secular pursuits and ambition, and strengthen them for the crisis at the end of time.

2. Christ exhorts them to buy "white garments" to cover their nakedness. He has in mind righteous deeds that are the fruit of an active faith in Jesus (Rev. 14:12; 19:8). In contrast to the prized garments made from the famous black wool of the city, Jesus admonishes the church to purchase that clothing that alone can cover its nakedness. We note here a line of demarcation between the world and the kingdom. Thus we cannot follow the world's value system and, at the same time, pursue the kingdom of God. Success in the world demands moral and spiritual compromise in the church.

3. Christ urges them to purchase spiritual ointment. Here we may understand the eyesalve that the risen Lord offers the church as the healing power of the Holy Spirit, whose active ministry in the church serves an illuminating purpose (see Rev. 4:5).

Finally, Christ follows His counsel with a reminder that His chastising of them results from His love, and appeals to them to "be zealous and repent" (Rev. 3:19). The point continues in the following verse, which pictures the risen Lord knocking at the door. Some may see this in a threatening way as a note of warning, and perhaps there is some truth here, since it forms part of the Laodicean message. But we should not overlook another dimension. Revelation presents a picture of the pleading Christ, a vision of the seeking God that comes through most clearly. William Holman Hunt's famous painting *The Light of the World* depicts the door of the human heart with no handle on the outside, indicating that the door can be opened only from within. This sums up Christ's counsel to Laodicea, for what He desires most and what they most need is for the believers there to invite the risen Lord into their midst so that His presence governs their life and ministry. For the gold, the garments, and the eyesalve He alone can and will provide at their request and in response to His invitation.

The message ends on a positive note. Christ promises to those who overcome the honor of sitting with Him and His Father on His throne (verse 21). And that is something that all the gold, and all the beautiful garments, and all the medical prescriptions in the world cannot provide.

---

[1] Ramsay, *The Letters to the Seven Churches*, p. 379.

[2] Barclay, *The Revelation of John*, vol. 1, pp. 114, 115.

[3] Finegan, *The Archeology of the New Testament*, p. 175.

[4] *The SDA Bible Commentary*, Ellen G. White Comments, vol. 7, p. 959.

[5] *The SDA Bible Commentary*, vol. 7, p. 756.

[6] Barclay, p. 118.

[7] Some suggest that both events are meant (*The SDA Bible Commentary*, vol. 7, p. 756).

[8] See Ellen G. White, *The Great Controversy*, p. 491.

[9] See Barclay, p. 121.

[10] Ramsay tells of the custom of Roman citizens wearing pure white togas on holidays and at religious ceremonies, and suggests that John may also have had in mind the idea of the citizens walking in triumph with the victorious General, while mourners and criminals would wear dirty and dark-colored togas (Ramsay, pp. 386, 387).

[11] Mounce, in *The Book of Revelation*, p. 115.

[12] Kittel, *Theological Dictionary of the New Testament*, vol. 1, pp. 101, 102; *The Interpreter's Dictionary of the Bible*, vol. E-J, p. 616.

[13] Mounce, p. 116.

[14] Ramsay, p. 406.

[15] *The SDA Bible Commentary*, Ellen G. White Comments, vol. 7, p. 961.

[16] For an excellent study that refutes the claims of a pretribulation rapture, see George E. Ladd, *The Blessed Hope*. Passages pertinent to our text appear on pages 85, 86.

[17] Revelation 14:6-11 is a message of warning to the unredeemed.

[18] Of the Philadelphia church, Ramsay writes: "It was always in dread of the last *hour of trial*, and was always *kept from* it. It stood like a pillar, the symbol of stability and strength. In the Middle Ages it struggled on, a small and weak city against a nation of warriors, and did not deny the Name, but was patient to the end; and there has been written on its history a name that is imperishable, so long as heroic resistance against overwhelming odds, and persevering self-reliance, when deserted by the world, are held in honour and remembered" (Ramsay, p. 412).

[19] Barclay, p. 137.

[20] See Mounce, p. 123.

[21] See Ford, *Revelation*, pp. 419, 420.

[22] Jacitus *Annals* 14. 27, in Barclay, p. 138.

[23] Ramsay, p. 419.

[24] See Ford, p. 420.

[25] Barclay, p. 140.

[26] Mounce, p. 125.

God's Holiness
in Awesome Array

(Based on Revelation 4)

"Worship the Lord in holy array; tremble before him, all the earth!" (Ps. 96:9).

The Throne Room (Rev. 4:1, 2) The scene changes from the churches on earth to the sanctuary in heaven. As we examine the opening verses of Revelation 4 we note two things that connect the earthly scene with the heavenly one: 1. The reference to the "open door." In the previous chapter Christ knocks at the door of the human heart (Rev. 3:20). The door is closed, indicating the condition of the Laodicean believers, who in their self-conceit and spiritual delusion see no need for divine help. The situation was considerably different, however, in the Philadelphian church. To the faithful there, Christ says that He has set before them an "open door, which no one is able to shut" (verse 8). The open door represents the limitless resources of God's grace that the loving Lord makes available as high priest and sovereign ruler.

The open door in heaven expresses two things about God: a. He is forever accessible to His church. Being in a world darkened by human sin and wickedness may tempt the believer to feel abandoned by God. And trials may press him into despair over God's apparent absence. But the risen Lord has opened the way to the Father, and the believer may rest in the assurance that no one can shut the open door to God's throne room.

b. God extends a continual invitation to sinful humanity. It is no coincidence that the door from earth to heaven is not shut. Heaven's openness to the sinner is the result of God's saving work in Jesus, which took place in accordance with the divine plan (1 Peter 1:20; Eph. 1:5-12). The Lord manifests His continual nature of eager invitation not only in His redemptive acts but also in the revelation of His holy will and purpose to the church. A voice invites John to "come up" and see "what must take place" (Rev. 4:1).

2. The reference to God's throne. In His message to the church in Laodicea, Christ promises to the overcomer the reward of sharing His throne (Rev. 3:21). The throne that Christ refers to in this instance is the victor's throne. The biblical picture suggests a couch similar to those in the throne rooms of Eastern monarchs rather than a single seat such as we find in the West. [1] In the throne room vision, John sees only One seated (Rev. 4:2). Here the prophet focuses on God's supreme majesty and the adoration that His divine self-disclosure awakens. The throne of God appears frequently throughout the book of Revelation, and serves to assure Christians that the Sovereign of the universe is in control however bleak the outlook may appear. The vision of the enthroned God directs attention from the transitory world to the eternal one, and provides the reader with an opportunity to put his present predicament in proper perspective.

The Vision of God Enthroned (Rev. 4:3)   John tells us that he was "in the Spirit" when he saw God seated on the throne (verse 2). He used the same expression in his introduction to his vision of the risen Lord (Rev. 1:10). By this he makes clear to his readers that what he saw and heard took place through the work of the Holy Spirit. It was not something he imagined or envisioned through his mind's eye. The mental state he found himself in resulted from divine initiative and was not something the prophet had induced in himself through meditation. The reference to a voice speaking to him like a trumpet (Rev. 4:1) recalls another feature of the initial vision (Rev. 1:10).

The prophet describes God seated on the throne in language drawn from Ezekiel 1:26-28. Like Ezekiel's description, John's portrait of the Deity in symbolic imagery heightens the sense of God's holiness. John employs the names of three precious stones—jasper, carnelian (sardius), and emerald—to convey the majestic presence of God, the brilliance that emanates from His throne. The scene brings to mind the psalmist's characterization of God as one enveloped in light (Ps. 104:2), and the apostle Paul's portrayal of Him as dwelling "in unapproachable light" (1 Tim. 6:16). The three stones formed part of the high priest's breastplate, representing certain Israelite tribes (Ex. 28:17-21). Jasper and carnelian were the last and the first stones, respectively, standing for Benjamin (the youngest of Jacob's sons) and Reuben (the eldest), respectively, and emerald appeared fourth on the breastplate, symbolizing Judah. It is also of interest to note that Ezekiel includes carnelian, jasper, and emerald among the stones that were part of Lucifer's adornment (Eze. 28:13), and that John identifies these same stones in the foundations of the New Jerusalem (Rev. 21:19, 20).

A rainbow surrounds the throne. The Genesis account of the Flood has the rainbow signifying God's covenant promise to Noah and to the generations following him that He would never again destroy the world by a flood (Gen. 9:8-17). The rabbis elaborated on the concept of the rainbow, offering different interpretations of its religious significance. Some saw it as an indication of divine censure, while others recognized it as a manifestation of divine glory.[2] John may have incorporated both views. To the believers the rainbow provides assurance of God's faithfulness, whereas to the wicked it points to the coming judgment.

The 24 Elders (Rev. 4:4)   The prophet sees 24 elders, wearing white garments and golden crowns, seated on thrones ranged around God's throne. Opinions differ widely as to the identity of the elders.[3] Such extensive speculation stems from their frequent mention in the book of Revelation (Rev. 4:4, 10; 5:5, 6, 8, 11, 14; 7:11, 13; 11:16; 14:3; 19:4). Various views have interpreted the elders as angels, men, wise men, prophets, or representatives of the redeemed. The principal role of the elders in the heavenly court is one of offering continuous adoration and praise to God and to the Lamb (Rev. 4:10, 11; 5:11, 12, 14; 7:11, 12; 11:16; 19:4). But they also serve an intercessory role. John sees them holding golden bowls of incense, which represent the prayers of the saints (Rev. 5:8). The fact that the elders remain constantly in God's presence suggests that they keep before Him the prayers of His people. One of the elders brings encouragement to John (verse 5), and another serves as interpreter of one of the visions (Rev 7:13-17).

The available evidence rejects the position that interprets the 24 elders as "an exalted angelic order,"[4] serving as the heavenly counterpart to the priestly and Levitical orders (see 1 Chron. 24-26). Instead, I believe we should see them as a special group selected from redeemed humanity. Such a view rests on the following deductions: 1. Their white garments testify to the purity of their lives as a result of the transforming power of the gospel. They must be part of the redeemed, who have "washed their robes" in the "blood of the Lamb" (Rev. 7:14). 2. The golden crowns on the heads of the elders are victors' crowns (the Greek work is *stephanos*), signifying their moral and spiritual triumph over evil through faith in Christ Jesus. Were the crowns to indicate royal status, we would expect John to have used the Greek word *diadema*, as he does when referring to Jesus as king of kings (Rev. 19:12, 16). 3. The number 24 may represent the entire body of believers, from the 12 tribes of Israel (God's people before the cross) and from the church or new Israel (God's people after the cross) as typified by the 12 apostles). [5] It may also allude to the 24 courses of the priesthood of ancient Israel as well, but it does not point to a heavenly counterpart of angels. It makes better sense to see here a reference to the priestly status of the redeemed, which John introduces us to in his salutation (Rev. 1:6).

The Seven Spirits of God (Rev. 4:5)   John has already introduced to us "the seven spirits" of God stationed before His throne (Rev. 1:4). But here the prophet depicts them as "seven torches of fire" that burn before the throne. Some have speculated that the seven torches are the seven golden lampstands, and concluded that the open door enabled John to look into the first compartment of the heavenly sanctuary. But we have nothing to warrant such a conclusion. Moreover, it ignores John's own interpretation in Revelation 4:5, which links the seven torches with the "seven spirits." More consistent with his view is the idea that the seven torches may describe another aspect of the Holy Spirit's work, namely, to reveal the holiness of the Divine Presence. The story of Moses' call has God manifesting His holiness in a burning bush unconsumed by the flames (Ex. 3:2-6). On the day of Pentecost the Holy Spirit descended upon the disciples in the form of fiery tongues (Acts 2:1-4) and anointed them with the divine credentials for ministry. Fire serves to symbolize the awesome character of God's presence or His holiness.

When they stood on the borders of the Promised Land, Moses warned the Israelites against idolatry by reminding them that their God is a "devouring fire" (Deut. 4:24). And the book of Hebrews admonishes us to learn from the lessons of Israel's history (see Heb. 12:25) and offer to God acceptable worship, for God is a "consuming fire" (verses 28, 29). Worship is an awed response to the revealed holiness of God. Since this is the theme of Revelation 4, an interpretation of the seven torches of fire as the Holy Spirit in the context of worship would be consistent with this fact.

Along with the seven torches of fire, John sees issuing from the throne flashes of lightening, and he hears voices and peals of thunder. He uses similar imagery elsewhere to describe the manifestation of divine wrath against the wicked (Rev. 8:5; 16:18). It is important to note that God reveals His wrath when He discloses His holy displeasure toward sin. The same holiness that draws believers into the experience of worship drives the infidels away in terror. The purging power of God's presence purifies His people, while it at the same time destroys the wicked.

The Sea of Glass (Rev. 4:6)   Next John sees spread out before the throne what looks like a sea of dazzling crystal. The symbolism makes sense when viewed against the background of several Old Testament passages: 1. In the wheel-within-a-wheel vision of Ezekiel, the prophet views above the heads of the living creatures what appears to be an expanse of firmament, "shining like crystal," and above that a throne (Eze. 1:22, 26). We find a similar picture of the firmament in the poetic speech of Elihu, one of Job's friends. Elihu depicts the sky as a hard "molten mirror" (Job 37:18). 2. The psalmist paints in picturesque language the scene of the celestial sea upon which God laid the beams of His chambers (Ps. 104:3). The symbolism suggests that the writer has in mind the place of God's throne. The idea of a celestial sea appears also in the Genesis account of Creation. When God created the heavenly expanse, He divided the waters below the firmament from those above it (Gen. 1:7).

The sea of glass is a "visual phenomenon which adds to the awesome splendor" of God's majesty.[6] This sea may symbolize the blinding light of His holiness and the immense distance, between God and the world, resulting from that holiness.[7] The expression "sea of glass" occurs again in Revelation 15, where the redeemed appear with their harps and offer to God their praise for the victory they received over the beast and its image (verses 2, 3). Finally, we note the reference to the "river of the water of life, bright as crystal, flowing from the throne of God and of the Lamb" (Rev. 22:1). The life-giving properties that flow from God's throne exhibit the same dazzling purity as that of the radiance emanating from His presence. The throne thus symbolizes the Source who provides all blessings and sustains all life.

The Four Living Creatures (Rev. 4:6-8)   The four living creatures offer difficulties to the interpreter just as do the 24 elders. While the book often mentions them, we lack sufficient information to identify them with any certainty. They seem to be patterned after a vision in Ezekiel. The Old Testament prophet's vision of the four living creatures describes each of them as having four faces (Eze. 1:4-14), whereas in Revelation each has only one face. In Ezekiel's vision the creatures may be upholding the firmament (see Eze. 1:22, 23), whereas in Revelation they always appear before God's throne in constant praise and worship (Rev. 4:6, 8; 5:6, 9, 14; 7:11; 19:4). They also perform duties associated with God's judgment in the last days. At their command the events depicted in the vision of the first four of the seven seals take place (Rev. 6:1, 3, 5, 7). One of them hands over to the seven angels the golden bowls that contain the seven last plagues (Rev. 15:7).

While we find definite differences between John's vision and that of Ezekiel's, the similarities are sufficient to warrant the conclusion that the four living creatures in both visions are the same. In Ezekiel's vision, moreover, we can identify the creatures with the cherubim surrounding God's throne: "These were the living creatures . . . ; and I knew that they were cherubim" (Eze. 10:20). From other Old Testament passages we gain a clearer picture of the work of this angelic order. In the wilderness sanctuary, representations of cherubim were on the veil that separated the Most Holy Place from the Holy Place (Ex. 26:31), and on the mercy seat (the ark) in the Most Holy Place (Ex. 25:18-21). Solomon's Temple depicted them in the Most Holy Place and on walls and doors (1 Kings 6:23-32; 2 Chron. 3:7). Cherubim were in the place of prayer, or the throne room, of the heavenly sanctuary (see 2 Kings 19:15). Two psalms describe God as enthroned upon the cherubim (Ps. 80:1; 99:1; see Isa. 37:16, where Hezekiah in prayer speaks of God enthroned above the cherubim), and one psalm portrays Him as flying on a cherub and on the wings of the wind (Ps. 18:10). And it was the cherubim who, at the entrance to the Garden of Eden, guarded the way to the tree of life (Gen. 3:24).

The four living creatures that surround God's throne in John's vision, then, are the cherubim, an exalted order of angels who serve closest to God as the guardians of His throne, and lead the heavenly hosts in adoration and praise.

We may ask why John, and Ezekiel before him, did not simply identify the four living creatures as cherubim. The answer appears in the symbolic imagery itself. Commentators generally recognize that the four living creatures signify "everything that is noblest, strongest, wisest, and swiftest in nature."[8] When we view it this way, we may understand the four living creatures as representatives of the entire order of creation, and thus offering on behalf of all living things supreme worship to God. In the Psalms we note references to nature's praise of God (Ps. 19:1, 2; 97:1, 6), and a summons to all creation to sing God's praises (Ps. 98:4-9; 148; 150). Through the constant praise of the four living creatures we see the heavenly counterpart to what the psalmist exhorts the earth to do.

As early as the second century of the Christian era, we find the first and fullest attempt to interpret the symbolism of the four living creatures. Irenaeus held that they "represented four aspects of the work of Jesus Christ, which in turn are represented in the four Gospels." [9] William Barclay summarizes various identifications this way: [10]

The scheme of Irenaeus	The scheme of Victorinus
Matthew—the man	Matthew—the man
Mark—the eagle	Mark—the lion
Luke—the ox	Luke—the ox
John—the lion	John—the eagle
The scheme of Athanasius	The scheme of Augustine
Matthew—the man	Matthew—the lion
Mark—the ox	Mark—the man
Luke—the lion	Luke—the ox
John—the eagle	John—the eagle

Worship in Heaven (Rev. 4:8-11)   The chapter reaches its conclusion on an exclamation of praise that falls into two parts: 1. Praise from the four living creatures. Day and night they offer their ceaseless praise to God. It is a doxology arising from their recognition of His awesome holiness, unlimited power, and everlasting nature, all attributes unique to the Deity, and thus forming the basis of endless adoration.

2. The worship of the 24 elders. Their worship comes in response to the praise of the four living creatures, and consists of their falling down in obeisance and casting their crowns before God's throne in humble submission. During Roman times defeated kings would throw their crowns before the bust of the Roman emperor as a sign of complete submission. The act of submission on the part of the elders signifies their absolute surrender to the sovereignty of One who has redeemed them from bondage and made them victorious over all evil powers. It is thus a loving response of gratitude and praise.

The 24 elders' ascription of praise has two aspects: 1. He is Lord and God. The title expresses the conviction that God alone is preeminent. It takes on added significance when we consider the fact that it was also the official title of Domitian, the Roman emperor, and that Christians who refused to acknowledge him as lord and god met an early death. Here the representatives of all believers offer their confession of faith in an exclamation of praise that anticipates that day when the entire body of believers will boldly proclaim that the Lord alone is God. 2. He is Creator. By virtue of this fact the Lord is incomparable. He created all things in heaven and on earth and therefore is worthy of all praise. Everything and everyone owe their existence to Him.

The doxology of the four living creatures, combined with that of the 24 elders, expresses the praise of the whole of creation and the church. In this sense we may say that it satisfies the exhortation of the psalmist in the concluding verse of the Psalter: "Let everything that breathes praise the Lord!" (Ps. 150:6). John wrote the book of Revelation in anticipation of the day when this will indeed take place.

[1] Barclay, *The Revelation of John*, vol. 1, p. 148.

[2] Ford, *Revelation*, p. 71.

[3] *Ibid.*, p. 72.

[4] Mounce, in *The Book of Revelation*, p. 137.

[5] See *The SDA Bible Commentary*, vol. 7, p. 768.

[6] Mounce, p. 136.

[7] See Barclay, p. 156.

[8] *Ibid.*, p. 159.

[9] *Ibid.*, p. 161.

[10] *Ibid.*, pp. 160, 161.

The Lion and
the Lamb Exalted

(Based on Revelation 5)

"At the name of Jesus every knee should bow, in heaven and on earth and under the earth." (Philippians 2:10).

The Scroll With the Seven Seals (Rev. 5:1)   Revelation 5 continues the throne room vision that John described in the previous chapter. He sees in the right hand of the Almighty a scroll with seven seals. At the outset, John focuses our attention on the scroll. The fact that it rests in God's hand indicates that it is a document of great importance, and its being sealed with seven seals suggests the sensitive nature of its contents and therefore the need to keep it secret. We have information from the Bible and other sources that sheds light on the subject.

1. Ezekiel's vision of the written scroll (Eze. 2:8—3:3). The scroll that Ezekiel saw contained "words of lamentation and mourning and woe." Like the document in John's vision, it had writing on the front and on the back, but the prophet makes no reference to seals. Instead, he receives instructions to eat the scroll (see Rev. 10:8-11), and upon doing so, found it to be "as sweet as honey" in his mouth.

2. The angel Gabriel's instruction to Daniel (Dan. 12:4, 9). After explaining the meaning of the time prophecies, Gabriel directs the prophet to seal up the message revealed to him. Before God sets up His kingdom, there will occur a time of trouble unprecedented in human history. But despite its severity, God will deliver His people—that is, every one "whose name shall be found written in the book" (Dan. 12:1). For the present, however, Gabriel tells the prophet to "shut up the words, and seal the book," the idea being that the words of the prophecy were meant for the people who would face the tribulation of the last days. The end-time will see an increase in human activity and knowledge (verse 4) and a readiness for the prophecies.

In Revelation 1:3 John alludes to the passage in Daniel. After introducing the message as the "revelation of Jesus Christ," the prophet stresses the importance of reading, hearing, and obeying it by issuing a threefold blessing and by pointing out that "the time is near." John wants his readers to know that the revelation disclosed to him and which he is passing on to them contains instruction for God's people in the last days. That which was at one time sealed is about to be disclosed. The revelator anticipates in vision, then, the unsealing of the scroll and the revealing of its contents.

In apocalyptic literature God entrusts His revelation to the prophet who then passes it on to God's people in written form. This enables the church to read, study, and reflect on the instruction carefully. Intense persecution makes the church less likely to hear the prophet's preaching or to listen to oral instruction. Therefore the written word of prophecy replaces the spoken word. The sealed scroll that John sees is a written document, a point that adds significance to the written word as a medium of divine communication.

As we noted earlier, John uses a composite of Old Testament passages to describe what he sees and experiences in vision, and under divine inspiration gives new meaning to the symbolism. Thus we find in the book of Revelation references and allusions to passages from Israelite law, history, wisdom, hymnody, and prophecy. We also observe John combining different literary forms such as the epistolary greeting and salutation in the introduction to the book (Rev. 1:4-8), his modification of the prophetic formula ("thus says the Lord") in the introductory words of the letters to the seven churches (Rev. 2:1, 8, 12, 18; 3:1, 7, 14), the priestly blessing (Rev. 1:3; 14:13; 19:9; 20:6; 22:7, 14), the formulas common in apocalyptic writings to introduce visions such as, "I turned to see" (Rev. 1:12) or "I looked, and lo" (Rev. 4:1) or "I saw" (Rev. 5:1), and so on. The book of Revelation is thus steeped in the language and literature of the Old Testament and at the same time has a message that is more than the sum of the Jewish Scriptures. It has a distinctive Christian character, despite its marked Jewish tone.

The Challenge of the Strong Angel (Rev. 5:2-4) John's interest in the scroll heightens with the demand of the strong angel: "Who is worthy to open the scroll and break its seals?" The angel proclaims his question with a loud voice so as to reach the ends of the universe, thus adding drama to a scene already tense with expectation. The prophet does not identify the strong angel, but we meet him again in Revelation 10:1 and 18:1. It is sheer speculation to suggest that Gabriel has this role, but the idea has some merit. Whoever he is, the angel's challenge goes unanswered. No one "in heaven or on earth or under the earth" is found worthy. Nobody in the entire universe meets the requirements or has the qualifications to disclose the contents of the divine document.

In the previous chapter John informed us that a voice summoned him to the door of heaven, and at that time he received a promise that he would see those things about to transpire (Rev. 4:1). The sealed scroll was about to be opened. Now the promise appears to be thwarted, and John weeps. To grasp the significance of his disappointment, we must recognize what a delay in the disclosure would mean to him and the church. In the introduction to the book John informs us that the Roman authorities had banished him to the island of Patmos because of his faithful witness to the truth. He writes to encourage his fellow believers to endure the hard times patiently because their deliverance nears. But to those weak in faith the thought of a delay could be crushing.

The sealed scroll contained the knowledge of God's holy will, and thus a disclosure of its contents would make known God's saving plan for His church. So long as the scroll remained sealed, the plan for the church in the end-time would remain a mystery. Here we note how closely interlaced God's revelatory and redemptive work are. God reveals what must shortly take place because He desires to prepare His people for the final assault of the enemy. A prepared church is an informed church. And a prepared church will go through the tribulation triumphantly, whereas one surprised by the enemy will more likely fail. John thus weeps at the prospect of a delay. In the prophet's grief we may see an allusion to the question raised by Daniel: "O my lord, what shall be the issue of these things?" Daniel does not get an answer but the angel tells him instead that "the words are shut up and sealed until the time of the end" (Dan. 12:8, 9). The idea that something has postponed God's final and decisive action indefinitely now devastates John. The incident dramatizes the dilemma in order to magnify the risen Lord because the glorified Christ will meet the challenge of the strong angel.

The Lion of Judah and the Root of David (Rev. 5:5)   One of the 24 elders consoles John with the assuring words that "the Lion of the tribe of Judah, the Root of David" can open the scroll and its seven seals because of His mighty victory over the forces of evil. The challenge of the strong angel thus becomes purely rhetorical, and forms an integral part of the worship scene introduced in the previous chapter. Psalm 24, a processional psalm celebrating the military triumph of the king (who serves as the vassal of the Lord), illustrates how the worship service may effectively employ a rhetorical question. The pertinent material appears in verses 7-10.

> Lift up your heads, O gates!
>> and be lifted up, O ancient doors!
>> that the King of glory may come in.
>
> Who is the King of glory?
>> The Lord, strong and mighty,
>> the Lord, mighty in battle!
>
> Lift up your heads, O gates!
>> and be lifted up, O ancient doors!
>> that the King of glory may come in.
>
> Who is the King of glory?
>> The Lord of hosts,
>> he is the King of glory!

As the king approaches the capital city, the cry goes forth, "Lift up your heads, O gates . . . that the King of glory may come in." A challenge greets the command: "Who is the King of glory?" And the question evokes a greater chord of enthusiasm: "The Lord, strong and mighty . . . !" Repeated again, the challenge produces an outburst of reverential praise. The temple used the psalm in its liturgy to celebrate the victory God achieved for His people through His anointed servant. [1] Scholars thus refer to it as a Messianic psalm, and the church understands it to have its ultimate fulfillment in Jesus. In Jesus the Anointed One, God has defeated the enemies of His church in a final way.

The challenge of the strong angel of Revelation 5 thus heightens the expectation of the heavenly congregation, whose ceaseless praise echoes throughout the cosmic courts and prepares the way for the ritual exaltation of the Lamb. The elder's words seek to comfort John, since the angel's challenge was not intended to cause grief. The appropriate response is one of joy and celebration. As to who is worthy to open the sealed scroll, the answer is clear. The risen Lord by virtue of His glorious triumph over death and the powers of evil, and through His supreme obedience to God, is indeed worthy. All heaven knows this fact. The angel's challenge provides the occasion to rejoice once again in the victory of the mighty King.

In his consolation to John, the elder ascribed to Christ two titles derived from the Old Testament: 1. He is the Lion of Judah. The designation recalls Jacob's final blessing of his sons in which he refers to Judah as "a lion's whelp" (Gen. 49:9). Later Jewish thought saw Messianic meaning in the appellation.[2] The imagery implies the lion's strength and the reputation the animal earned because of it. As folklore credits the lion with being the king of beasts, Jesus is king of earthly rulers. The title appropriately points to the awesome manifestation of God's power in Christ's conquest, and emphatically asserts Jesus to be the all-powerful Messiah who alone is worthy to open the scroll and reveal to the universe the destiny of the world.

2. He is the Root of David. The designation derives from a Messianic prophecy of Isaiah and echoes the verses that speak of the coming king as "a shoot from the stump of Jesse" (Isa. 11:1). Jesse was the father of David, Israel's greatest king. The prophet foresees another David arising to lead the armies of God's people successfully in battle against the enemy and reestablish Israel's sovereignty in the world. The prophecy found its fulfillment in Jesus Christ's triumphant death and resurrection, and will be made evident in the last day when Christ sets up His kingdom of glory and peace.

The Lamb Exalted (Rev. 5:6, 7) The central act in the vision's drama goes to the risen Lord, depicted here as a lamb standing upright with sacrificial scars. It has seven horns and seven eyes representing the seven Spirits of God. The image of the lamb has a rich religious symbolism in both the Old and New Testaments, and a brief summary of Israel's traditions will clarify the meaning of what John sees in vision.

1. The Paschal lamb associated with the exodus from Egypt (Ex. 12:1-28). The slain lamb served as a substitute for Israel's firstborn, and its blood on the doorpost notified the avenging angel to pass over the house and spare the family. The Passover meal provided Israel with an opportunity to preserve the memory of that night when God delivered them from Egyptian bondage. This was the meal that Jesus observed with His disciples on the night of His betrayal, and one that He transformed into a memorial service pointing back to His sacrificial death (Matt. 26:17-29; 1 Cor. 11:23-26). The application is quite clear. Jesus suffered the death that we deserve in order to

liberate us from sinful bondage to Satan. And it is His saving sacrifice that sustains the church through tribulation in the last days. For it is the victory He achieved through His death that authorizes Him to open the scroll and reveal its contents. And this revelatory event has redemptive value in that it provides enlightenment and renewed hope to the church. The Lamb that was slain is the risen Lord who will lead His people through the struggles of the last days.

2. The lamb offered in the daily services of the sanctuary (Ex. 29:38-42). The dominant sacrificial victim, it stood for innocence, purity, gentleness, and meekness. In his prophetic poem of the Suffering Servant, Isaiah draws from the language of sacrifice when he depicts the servant as "a lamb that is led to the slaughter" (Isa. 53:7). He was wounded, bruised, and chastised for our sins, and through His suffering we find healing (Isa. 53). The New Testament understands and explains the death of Jesus against the background of Old Testament sacrificial practices (Heb. 9, 10), and points to Him as the spotless Lamb of God (1 Peter 1:19) who takes away the sin of the world (John 1:29, 36).

In each example the word used for lamb is *amnos*, whereas in the book of Revelation John prefers the word *arnion*. When we consider the fact that *arnion* does not appear elsewhere in the New Testament, and that the book of Revelation uses it 28 times in reference to Jesus, we find ourselves compelled to look more closely at this symbolic representation of the risen Lord. In doing so, we note two things: 1. The Lamb bears the marks of sacrifice. John draws from the wealth of Israel's sacrificial traditions to point to the glorious victory that Jesus has achieved on Calvary. The church must never lose sight of the suffering that Christ endured on behalf of sinners. It must also understand its own suffering against the background and in the light of Christ's sacrifice. The way to the kingdom is by the way of the cross.

2. The Lamb has seven horns and seven eyes. The marks of sacrifice point to Christ's victory in the past, and to present benefits that the church will receive from that eternal accomplishment. The seven horns and seven eyes indicate the present work of Christ on behalf of the struggling church. Once again we may appeal to the Old Testament to aid our understanding of John's symbolism. a. In Israel the horn stood for two things: first, it represented power. The blessing of Moses refers to the horns of Joseph as it compares the tribe to an aggressive wild ox that uses its horns to push other occupants off the land. According to

Moses, the tribes of Ephraim and Manasseh—descendants of
Joseph—will successfully guard their territory and push peoples
to the ends of the earth (Deut. 33:17). To dramatize his particular
prediction, the prophet Zedekiah made iron horns to signify the
triumph he envisioned over the Syrian forces (1 Kings 22:11). In
his vision of the four beasts, Daniel describes the fourth beast as
"terrible and dreadful and exceedingly strong" and adds that it
had 10 horns (Dan. 7:7). His vision of the ram and the he-goat has
the he-goat breaking the two horns of the ram, leaving the ram
with "no power" (Dan. 8:7). At the peak of his power, his own
horn breaks and four horns come up in its place (verse 8). The
horn thus represents the military might and the political power
of earthly kings. The Lamb with seven horns, then, signifies the
supreme might and power of the King of kings, whose absolute
sovereignty will soon manifest itself throughout the universe.
Viewed symbolically, the number seven points to Christ's om-
nipotence. He is the all-powerful Messiah who will lead His
church triumphantly through tribulation to the kingdom.

The horn also represented honor and exaltation. In a psalm
of praise celebrating God's faithful dealings with His people, the
psalmist exclaims, "Thou art the glory of their strength; by thy
favor our horn is exalted" (Ps. 89:17). The same psalm has God
promising to honor and exalt David and his offspring, stating that
in His name David's horn shall be exalted. The little horn in the
apocalyptic visions of Daniel abused its power by elevating itself
to a position of honor, committing unpardonable blasphemy
against God (Dan. 8:9-12). The seven horns of the Lamb in
Revelation 5, thus, symbolize the glorified state of the exalted
Christ.

b. The Lamb has seven eyes, which are the seven Spirits sent
throughout the earth. Once again we meet the seven Spirits of
God. The expression occurs in connection with the work of the
risen Lord. Whereas the seven horns depict Christ's omnipo-
tence, the seven eyes represent His omniscience. Jesus is the
all-powerful and all-wise Messiah. The imagery reflects one of
the visions of Zechariah. There an angel tells the prophet that the
seven lamps are "the eyes of the Lord, which range through the
whole earth" (Zech. 4:1-10). John wishes to communicate to us
the fact that nothing on earth escapes the eyes of the Lord. The
cruel injustices meted out against the innocent, the false testimony rendered in court, the moral compromises with the
enemy, do not take place in secret but in full view of the exalted

Christ. And someday everyone will face Him in judgment to give account for his misdeeds. It is a sober picture and, at the same time, an encouraging one for the faithful who suffer for Christ's sake.

John witnesses the Lamb stepping forward and taking the scroll from the right hand of God. It is the central act in the drama of worship, the anticipated response to the strong angel's challenge. The Lamb slain, the all-powerful, all-wise Messiah in His majesty and meekness alone, is the one worthy to open the scroll.

The Celestial Chorus (Rev. 5:8-14) The book of Revelation reverberates with praise. Our present passage remains unsurpassed in its description of worship and its expressed adoration and joy. The scene John depicts must have thrilled him beyond imagination. We observe a progressive development of acclamation in the celestial chorus. It begins and ends with the four living creatures and the 24 elders.

1. The praise of the creatures and elders. When the Lamb receives the sealed scroll, the four living creatures and the elders fall down before Him and break forth in spontaneous praise. We should note three things here: a. The elders have harps. The harp was the traditional instrument of Jewish worship, and many of the hymns in the Psalter were sung with the harp as an accompaniment. In the Psalms we find exhortations to praise the Lord with the harp (Ps. 33:2; 98:5; 147:7, KJV). It was the instrument of praise, and we find that fact reflected in the worship of heaven.

b. The elders have golden bowls of incense. The bowls are full of incense and symbolize the prayers of God's people. As representatives of the entire body of believers, the elders keep before the throne the expressed needs of the church, but they do not serve as priestly mediators, since that would stand in sheer contradiction to the direct access that Christ has achieved for His people. Instead we are to see the elders as a human symbol of the church, anticipating the day when the people of God of all ages will be present to sing His praises in person.

c. The elders and the living creatures sing a new song. The phrase *a new song* appears frequently in the book of Psalms, and has a close association with Israel's religious experience. The new song may be a hymn of praise for God's work as Creator (Ps. 33:4-9) or for His protection (verses 10-17). It may be a song of praise for a specific healing (Ps. 40:3), for God's saving deeds in history (Ps. 96:1-6), for a victory in battle (Ps. 98:1-3), or for deliverance from the hand of the enemy (Ps. 144:9-11). Or the new song may simply be an exultation in response to the Lord's faithfulness to His people (Ps. 149:1-9).

It is an inspiration to attend a religious concert and hear trained voices sing God's praises. But how much more uplifting it is to participate in a congregational choir whose praise to God overflows with gratitude for specific blessings in the life situation of the church.

The four living creatures and the elders burst forth with a hymn extolling the Lamb for His great redemptive act. It focuses on the benefits He provides through His saving death. By His blood He purchased the church for God—a church consisting of peoples from all parts of the world (Rev. 5:9). And by His blood He made a kingdom and priests to God from the people He redeemed from sin (verse 10). Of interest to us is the objective of Christ's redemptive work. He purchased us from sin and set us free so that we may live to sing God's praises. The saints have been saved for God's kingdom, to walk in the light of His glory, and to exclaim thanksgiving in His courts for what He has done through Jesus Christ His Son.

2. The praise of the angels. John witnesses in vision a throng of countless angels. Following the song of the living creatures and the elders, they raise their voice in loud acclamation, "Worthy is the Lamb who was slain, to receive power and wealth and wisdom and might and honor and glory and blessing" (verse 12). Their sevenfold ascription of praise enumerates the attributes of the exalted Christ. Jesus manifested each one during His earthly ministry on behalf of others, but never was He self-serving. The host of angels now break forth in supreme adoration to honor and worship the One who has won their deepest loyalty and love.

3. The praise of all creation. Beginning with the extolment of the living creatures, the music swells as a chorus of innumerable angels comes in, gradually becoming stronger and louder with reverential joy until the third wave of singers join in the holy veneration of the Lamb. The ripple of praise now becomes a tidal wave of adoration. All creatures in heaven and on earth and under the earth and in the sea can no longer contain themselves. They break forth with exuberance, saying, "To him who sits upon the throne and to the Lamb be blessing and honor and glory and might for ever and ever!" We were created to sing God's praises,

and in so doing we participate in God's glory and mature in the light of His presence.

Recently a young woman who had once been a member of a Seventh-day Adventist church felt convicted by the Holy Spirit to make amends and return to the Lord. She asked about attending church, but the members of her former congregation advised her against going back there. They told her that she would get little from the services, and that they themselves had stopped attending for that reason. So she came to me quite perplexed, since she felt convinced that she should begin to attend worship. My response to her was simple. God wants us to come to church to worship Him. He has summoned us to His house every week to bring our thanksgiving and praise. It is in giving to God that we receive a blessing. If we have no reason to attend church, if there is no motivation other than to get something for ourselves, if we have nothing to offer God, we should become alarmed over our spiritual condition, for we may well be on the verge of spiritual death.

4. The crescendo of praise ends with the response of the living creatures and the elders. In awesome homage the four living creatures say "Amen!" and the 24 elders prostrate themselves before the presence of God and the Lamb and again offer their worship. We thus have come full circle in the exaltation and magnification of the Lamb. For heaven's praise is ceaseless, and the gratitude of creation is eternal.

---

[1] Mitchell Dahood, *Psalms I, The Anchor Bible*, p. 151.

[2] Barclay, *The Revelation of John*, vol. 1, p. 169.

Vengeance Is God's Work

(Based on Revelation 6)

"For the time has come for judgment to begin with the household of God; and if it begins with us, what will be the end of those who do not obey the gospel of God?" (1 Peter 4:17).

The Opening of the Seven Seals The central act in Revelation 5 was that of the Lamb taking the scroll with the seven seals from the right hand of God seated on the throne. The present chapter focuses on the actual opening of the first six seals. John's visions of the sealing of God's servants and of the great multitude of saints appear between the sixth and seventh seals (Rev. 7). We should note that John does not reveal the contents of the scroll at the breaking of the seven seals. That awaits another time (Rev. 19:1–21:4).[1] Instead our attention centers on a series of events taking place in the church and in the world that disclose in a preliminary way God's redemptive and judicial purposes.

Some have understood Revelation 6 as the beginning of a holy war between the forces of good and the forces of evil.[2] Through the sequence of the seals, trumpets, and bowls (Rev. 6-16) we may see a dramatic portrayal of God's righteous judgments. Before commenting on the individual seals, we will consider several apocalyptic passages from the Scriptures that illuminate our understanding of John's vision.

1. The visions of Zechariah. The prophet observes horsemen and chariots of various colors (in Zechariah 1:8-17 he depicts a man riding a red horse, and behind him red, sorrel, and white horses, whereas in Zechariah 6:1-8 he sees red, black, white, and dappled gray-colored horses). Their colors are of no apparent significance to him, whereas to John the colors of the four horses characterize the work of the four horsemen: they conquer (white), shed blood (red), spread famine (black), and cause death (pale). Zechariah's visions have the four chariots as instruments of divine judgment, sent out from the Lord to patrol the earth,

but in John's vision the four horsemen execute God's holy will in the earth.

2. The eschatological discourse of Jesus. During His teaching on the last days Jesus told His disciples that before He returns there will come a time of great terrors (the birth pangs of the Messiah) for the church and the world (Luke 21:10-19). It will be a period of war when "nation will rise against nation, and kingdom against kingdom" (verse 10), resulting in great bloodshed as people "fall by the edge of the sword" (verses 23, 24). "Famines and pestilences" (verse 11) will strike, and humanity will face such distress and perplexity that men will faint with fear (verses 25, 26). God's people will encounter intense persecution in the form of court trials and imprisonment. Family and friends will betray them, and all will hate them because of their witness to the truth. Some will be put to death for their faith (verses 12-17).

We find many parallels between the signs of the last days in the discourse of Jesus and the events described in the vision of the seven seals. Jewish and early Christian thinking visualized a time of great trouble and unprecedented woe preceding the establishment of God's kingdom.

Seventh-day Adventists understand the seven seals as depicting events in history, beginning with the church in the first century of the Christian era and culminating with the eschatological judgment at the time of the Second Advent.[3]

The Four Horsemen (Rev. 6:1-8)   The four living creatures participate in the events depicted in the first four seals. When the Lamb breaks each seal, one of the creatures bids the horse and rider to come forth.[4] The first horse was white and its rider had a bow and a crown (*stephanos*, meaning a "victor's wreath"), and went forth "conquering and to conquer" (Rev. 6:2). The picture is one of conquest in war.

In the Old Testament the bow represents military power. When Jeremiah describes the destruction of Babylon, he tells of their warriors being taken captive and their bows broken in pieces, indicating military defeat (Jer. 51:56). Hosea announces divine judgment against the people of Israel by referring to God snapping "the bow of Israel" in the valley of Jezreel (Hosea 1:5). The psalmist speaks of God making wars cease by breaking the bow and shattering the spear (Ps. 46:9).

If John is following the vision of Zechariah, the four horses would stand for the four winds of heaven that God releases on earth with a destructive blast. The horses and their riders would represent the instruments of God's wrath, and point to the disintegrating conditions in world affairs that Jesus described in His discourse to His disciples.

Should the white horse stand for the church, however, the symbolism would not point to destructive forces at work in the world, but the advance of the gospel against the forces that oppose God's redemptive plan. It would portray a militant church triumphant in its witness to the Word of God and the testimony of Jesus. Consistent with the picture of a militant church is the portrait of Jesus in Revelation 19:11-16 as the conquering Messiah who on a white horse leads His armies (also on white horses) victoriously in battle.

Viewed as representing a period of church history, the white horse would stand for the apostolic age, a time when the gospel went to all the world and the church experienced its greatest spiritual conquests.

The second horse was bright-red and its rider had a great sword. He received permission to take peace from the earth and as a result caused great bloodshed. The vision sketches a picture of social chaos and disintegrating human relationships, of men and women turning against one another in satanic fury. In his pronouncement of doom against the nation of Egypt, Isaiah pictures God as stirring up the Egyptians so that they fight among themselves. Every man attacks his brother and his neighbor. City is pitted against city, and kingdom against kingdom (Isa. 19:1-4).

Zechariah depicts God's judgment against the enemies of His people in similar terms: "And on that day a great panic from the Lord shall fall on them, so that each will lay hold on the hand of his fellow, and the hand of the one will be raised against the hand of the other" (Zech. 14:13). Jesus warned that human wickedness would increase, causing "most men's love" to grow cold (Matt. 24:12). And the apostle Paul informed Timothy that in the last days men will be unholy, inhuman, implacable, treacherous, and reckless (2 Tim. 3:1-4). It is a time of terror when rage consumes the world, and people are bent on a course of destruction.

The color of the second horse corresponds with the mission of its rider and symbolizes a terrible slaughter. While the first horse and rider signifies invasion from without, the second horse and rider suggests internal strife. Applied to the church, the red horse points to a time of intense persecution. Jesus spoke of the tribulation coming upon the church, leading many to betray each other with venomous hatred (Matt. 24:9, 10).

A period of martyrdom followed the brilliant expansion of the church during the first century of the Christian Era. Some of the persecution came from the hands of certain elements of the Jews because of the inroads that Christians had made among the God-fearing Gentiles. And then pagan Rome launched a violent assault against the church toward the end of the first century. But eventually Christians would encounter abusive treatment from those within their ranks, as well as from family members and friends who did not share their religious convictions.

At the opening of the third seal a black horse appears and on it a rider with a balance in his hand. The balance was a cross-beam used in ancient times to measure grain. From the midst of the four living creatures a voice announces the price for a quart of wheat and three quarts of barley. The amount of food purchased for one denarius would be one person's ration for a day. The denarius was a Roman silver coin, and in John's time it represented approximately what a common laborer would earn in a day. When we compare the prices mentioned in the vision to the price of grain in Italy at that time, we see that the cost of wheat and barley has experienced heavy inflation—some estimates run as high as 16 times the normal price of grain.[5]

A voice warns against harming the oil and the wine. Grain, wine, and oil were the main crops in Palestine (Rev. 6:5, 6; Deut. 7:13; 11:14; 28:51; Hosea 2:8, 22). Because the olive tree and the grapevine had much deeper roots than the grain, they could survive a drought easier than wheat could.

The scene described here is one of famine. The vision does not explain its cause. But whether it resulted from drought or war, the point is that we must see the famine as a divine judgment signifying God's wrath against the wicked powers. The wheat and barley are available but at a prohibitive price. It would take a man's entire wages to buy enough grain for one person for a day. If the man had a family, it would not suffice. If instead of wheat, he would buy barley, a cheaper grain, he might stretch the supply for the family, but he would have nothing left for other necessities.

Viewed as symbolic of the church, the black horse represents a period of spiritual famine. Amos foretells of such a time when the Lord "will send a famine on the land; not a famine of bread, nor a thirst for water, but of hearing the words of the Lord" (Amos 8:11). Such a famine would occur when the church became preoccupied with material things.[6]

When the Lamb opened the fourth seal, John saw a horse as pale as a corpse. The rider's name was Death, and behind him came Hades. And they had authorization to destroy a fourth of the earth by means of the sword, famine, pestilence, and wild beasts. The devastation is horrible, but it does not represent global destruction, since only a fourth of mankind are slain. Once again John draws his imagery from the Old Testament. Ezekiel announces the coming doom against Jerusalem because of the unmitigated idolatry practiced there. God will send His "four sore acts of judgment" upon the city—sword, famine, evil beasts, and pestilence (Eze. 14:21). In Leviticus these four acts of divine judgment appear in a different order and arrangement.

God will respond to Israel's faithlessness in a series of punishments: First, He will send the wild beasts to attack their children and cattle, thus reducing their number considerably. If Israel refuses to repent, He will execute His vengeance with the sword. Should the people seek refuge in their cities instead of returning to the Lord, He will spread pestilence among them and deliver them into the hand of the enemy. And if they persist in their sins and harden their hearts, the Lord will cause them to eat the flesh of their sons and daughters, for their bread will not satisfy them (Lev. 26:21-29). In the series of judgments executed by the fourth horseman, some have seen "the progressive deterioration of civilization."[7] The ravages of the sword destroy human life and crops, leaving a community desolate and hungry. Because of their weakened state the survivors cannot fight off disease and pestilence. And when pestilence strikes, it takes its toll, leaving those who remain in a debilitated and helpless state, no longer able to protect themselves against the wild beasts.

The fourth horse depicts an extremely grim situation. The period of church history corresponding most closely to this picture is that of the Dark Ages, when the faithful suffered immensely at the hands of powerful leaders in church and state. The established Christian church had the appearance of being spiritually dead.

The Cry of the Martyrs (Rev. 6:9-11)   With the breaking of the fifth seal John observed in vision the souls of those who had died for their faith. The scene thus changes from earth to heaven, more specifically to the heavenly sanctuary. In Revelation 1 the prophet witnessed the exalted Christ among the golden lamp-stands, and in Revelation 4 he received an invitation to view God's sacred throne. Now he calls attention to the altar of sacrifice, corresponding to the altar of burnt offering in the earthly tabernacle (Ex. 27:1-8). When God instructed Moses to build the sanctuary, He provided him with a pattern of the one in heaven (Ex. 25:9, 40; Num. 8:4; Heb. 8:5; 9:23).

John saw the souls of the slain under the altar in the heavenly sanctuary. We must keep in mind the fact that his visions are cast in symbolic imagery, and that the Old Testament often provides the key that unlocks their meaning. In this case we must turn to the sacrificial ritual of Israel's sanctuary service to grasp the significance of what he witnessed.

The worshiper was taught that blood was the most sacred sacrificial element: "For the life of the flesh is in the blood; and I have given it for you upon the altar to make atonement for your souls; for it is the blood that makes atonement, by reason of the life" (Lev. 17:11). It was an important part of the ritual of sacrifice to take some of the blood of the animal and sprinkle it before the Lord in front of the veil separating the holy place from the Most Holy Place. In addition, the priest put blood on the horns of the altar of incense. And the rest of the blood he poured out at the base of the altar of burnt offering located in the outer court (Lev. 4:5-7).

Such Old Testament passages provide an important back-ground for our interpretation of the fifth seal. What John de-scribes in his portrayal of the souls of the martyrs is their faithful witness to the Word of God and the testimony of Jesus (Rev. 1:9). Using symbolism drawn from the ritual of sacrifice, the prophet depicts the martyrs giving themselves up to God. Their lifeblood has been poured out as an offering to Him.

The apostle Paul used similar imagery in reference to his ministry. In his letter to the Christians at Philippi, he writes, "Even if I am to be poured as a libation upon the sacrificial offering of your faith, I am glad and rejoice with you all" (Phil. 2:17). Paul waited in a Roman prison for his execution for his faith. Eventually he told Timothy, "For I am already on the point of being sacrificed; the time of my departure has come" (2 Tim. 4:6). Scripture does not view the death of the martyr as some-thing horrible or unhealthy, since it expresses to the world a positive witness for truth. It constitutes the supreme act of love and loyalty to God. In the light of God's promise of eternal life to the faithful, the martyr's death does not constitute a tragedy but a mighty triumph! Through his victorious death the martyr hands the enemy a devastating defeat.

At the same time we must also note the martyrs' cry: "O Sovereign Lord, holy and true, how long before thou wilt judge and avenge our blood on those who dwell upon the earth?" (Rev. 6:10).

1. The cry is an expression of faith. When we keep in mind the fact that we are dealing with symbolism, we avoid the pitfalls of a strictly literal interpretation. The picture in John's vision derives from the Genesis story of Cain slaying his brother Abel. When God addresses Cain in judgment, He declares, "The voice of your brother's blood is crying to me from the ground" (Gen. 4:10). Blood has no voice, and the dead cannot complain. Obviously the expressions are figurative and in this respect more effective than literal ones.

The shed blood points to an act of grave injustice. As the Sovereign Lord of the universe, God is concerned with acts of injustice, and will deal with them in His own way and time. But He takes special note of those crimes committed against His people. Abel represents the true worshiper, while Cain embodies the wicked who harm the righteous. In John's vision the martyrs cry out to God with the confidence that He will hear their prayer and vindicate them. Their shed blood witnesses to the violence done His people and now testifies in the heavenly court before the divine tribunal.

2. It is a plea for help. However strong our faith in God may be, we will continue to need the assurance that He is present, that He sees our affliction, that He hears our desperate plea for help, that He knows our suffering, and that He will act on our behalf without delay. The martyrs' supplication represents the cry of the righteous sufferer throughout human history. It is a request for strength to endure the ordeal of conflict. "How long, O Lord?" is the plea of the psalmist, who struggles in bewilderment over the wicked assaults against the righteous (Ps. 79:1-7). "O Lord, how long shall I cry for help?" the prophet Habakkuk exclaims as he witnesses the violence and destruction in Jerusalem (Hab. 1:1-4). "For how long?" Daniel asks the angel, must the blasphemy continue (Dan. 8:13)?

3. Finally, it is a demand for justice. We should not see it as a desire to get even or to take revenge, but an intense wish for God to vindicate Himself in the universe and bring the great

controversy between good and evil to an end. How long will God allow humanity to do injustices against His name, against His church, against His people? The cry is thus a complaint that anticipates a reply that will bring relief.

God makes a twofold response: 1. The martyrs receive a white robe, a symbol of their blessed state arising from their glorious victory over the enemy. Their faithful witness transformed the tragedy of death into a triumph resulting in life eternal. 2. Heaven tells the martyrs to rest a little longer. For the believer, death is not final but is compared to a condition of sleep (John 11:11-14; 25, 26). The death of the martyr is thus a blessed state of rest that God grants him until the end of the conflict. " 'Blessed are the dead who die in the Lord henceforth.' 'Blessed indeed', says the Spirit, 'that they may rest from their labors, for their deeds follow them!' " (Rev. 14:13).

The idea expressed in the instruction "to rest" is that the full quota of martyrs is needed to bring the conflict with evil to a close. The testimony of the martyrs whose souls John sees under the altar would be incomplete without the witness of others. We find a similar thought expressed in the book of Hebrews. Those who have endured martyrdom have not as yet received the promised inheritance because of the need of additional witnesses through whom God will perfect the testimony of His people (Heb. 11:39–12:2).

The Lamb's Wrath Against the Wicked (Rev. 6:12-17) When the Lamb tears open the sixth seal, John sees in vision a terrifying display of divine wrath against the wicked. The judgment disclosed dramatically displays not only God's displeasure toward evil, but also His desire to vindicate Himself and His people. The Lamb's wrath comes in response to the martyrs' cry for justice. The judgment scene that John here depicts, reveals several things. The Lamb's wrath brings about total catastrophe. John portrays this through a list of six phenomena, all of which consist of natural disasters. The same phenomena appear in other biblical passages focusing on the terrors of the end time. As in the case with John's vision, they view the chaos in nature not as the result of social conditions but as something brought about through divine intervention.

1. The quaking of the earth. Amos saw the coming earthquake as a sign of God's judgment (Amos 8:8). Ezekiel foretells a great shaking that affects the fish, the birds, the beasts, all creeping things, and finally the whole of humanity as well (Eze.

38:19, 20). We note a similar scene in the prophecies of Joel and Haggai (Joel 2:10; Haggai 2:6). In His Olivet discourse Jesus spoke of "earthquakes in various places" occurring as signs pointing to but preceding the end of the world (Matt. 24:7, 8).

2. The darkening of the sun and the moon. Using language similar to that employed by John, Isaiah depicts God blackening the sun, clothing it with sackcloth, the garment of those in mourning (Isa. 50:3). Joel predicts that before "the great and terrible day of the Lord comes," the moon will turn to blood (Joel 2:31), no longer reflecting the light from the sun (see also Matt. 24:29).

3. The falling of the stars. Isaiah graphically describes the descent of the stars in ominous colors. Before the stars take their plunge, they rot the way the corpses of the wicked will decay on the face of the ground, and then like dead leaves of the vine and the fig tree, they plummet from the sky (Isa. 34:2-4; Matt. 24:29). The natural phenomena signal the collapse of the created order.

4. The disappearing sky. Isaiah sees the sky roll up as a scroll after the rotting stars drop from it (Isa. 34:4). John draws his picture of the falling stars and the vanishing sky from this passage. It portrays the complete disintegration of the firmament at God's displeasure, and foreshadows the final judgment of the evil powers.

5. The removal of the mountains and the islands. They are natural symbols of stability and refuge. So complete is the destruction that even the mountains disappear, and the islands no longer offer a haven for the shipwrecked sailor. The prophets Jeremiah and Nahum speak of the mountains quaking and the hills melting from the intense heat of God's anger, leaving the world a global wasteland (Jer. 4:24; Nahum 1:5).

6. The devastating fear that drives humankind to despair. John names seven social classes to signify the universal judgment of the Lamb: the kings of the earth, great men, generals, the rich, the strong, the slave, and the free person. Regardless of social position, no one will escape the avenging wrath of the Lamb. In his prophecy of doom against Israel Amos lists seven classes of soldiers who meet defeat in battle, to indicate the complete annihilation of the army (Amos 2:14-16).

So desperate are the wicked that they cry out to the mountains and the rocks to cover them so that they might escape the visible manifestation of the Lamb's consuming anger. The revelator's imagery derives from Hosea 10:8 and Isaiah 2:10, 11;

19-21. The awesome presence of the Lamb evokes feelings of horror and dread among the wicked, who prefer death over facing Him in judgment: "The great day of their wrath has come, and who can stand before it?" (Rev. 6:17). The rhetorical question reminds one of those in the prophecies of Nahum: "Who can stand before his indignation? Who can endure the heat of his anger?" (Nahum 1:6); and Malachi: "Who can endure the day of his coming, and who can stand when he appears?" (Mal. 3:2).

---

[1] See Kenneth Strand, *Interpreting the Book of Revelation*, p. 57.

[2] Mounce, in *The Book of Revelation*, p. 151.

[3] *The SDA Bible Commentary*, Vol. 7, pp. 775, 776.

[4] *Ibid.*

[5] *Ibid.*, p. 777.

[6] *Ibid.*

[7] *Ibid.*

Sealed, Secured, and Saved

(Based on Revelation 7:1-8)

"Though I walk through the valley of the shadow of death, I fear no evil; for thou art with me" (Psalm 23:4).

The Vision of the Sealing of God's Servants   The vision of the sealing of God's servants is one of two visions that John inserts parenthetically between the sixth and seventh seals. Coming as it does after the terrifying scenes in the sixth seal, it provides a vivid contrast between the panic of the pagans and the security of the saints, and we may see it as an answer to the question, "Who can stand before the wrath of the Lamb?" The sealing of the servants has a saving purpose, namely to protect the saints from the destruction that awaits the earth. For only those with "the seal of the living God" (Rev. 7:2) will be able to stand in the day of the Lamb.

Revelation 7 treats the theme of the remnant. It is a motif that occurs again in Revelation 14, which introduces the sealed servants of God as those who "had been redeemed from the earth," who "have not defiled themselves with women," who "follow the Lamb wherever he goes," who "have been redeemed from mankind as first fruits for God and the Lamb," and in whose mouth "no lie was found" (Rev. 14:3-5).

Throughout the Bible the concept of the remnant appears in the context of God's work as Saviour and Judge of the earth. We find it, for example, in the story of Noah and the Flood. Human wickedness had reached catastrophic proportions. God instructed Noah to build an ark large enough for his family and a small portion of animal life. The ark served as a refuge from the wrath of God that came upon the world in the flood of waters: "He blotted out every living thing that was upon the face of the ground, man and animals and creeping things and the birds of the air; they were blotted out from the earth. Only Noah was left, and those that were with him in the ark" (Gen. 7:23).

The notion of "remnant" thus involves salvation and judgment. Those who belong to the remnant escape the judgment through God's saving intervention. They survive the terrors of the end-time not on their own merits but by the sheer grace of God. We may see His grace in the instruction He provides, as well as in His mighty acts of deliverance.

The Angels Holding the Winds of the Earth (Rev. 7:1) John noticed four angels standing at the four corners of the earth, holding back the four winds of destruction. The angels are agents of God whose work is to restrain the destructive forces until He seals His people. They prevent the wind from blowing on "earth or sea or against any tree." We do not hear about the four angels or the four winds again, but we have reason to believe that the destruction described in Revelation 8, following the sounding of the trumpets, results from the four angels releasing the four winds.

It is again important to remind ourselves that we are dealing with symbolic language. We should not, therefore, take the expression "the four corners of the earth" literally. However, it might be helpful to visualize the four points of the compass and the winds of destruction blowing diagonally across the earth from these specific points. In any case, it was not uncommon for Bible writers to speak of the "four corners of the earth" when they wished to describe the global impact of an event. Isaiah prophesies that the time will come when the Messiah will restore Israel to a position of preeminence in the world and will gather the outcasts of Israel and the dispersed of Judah from the four corners of the earth (Isa. 11:12). Ezekiel tells of the end coming upon "the four corners of the land" because of the people's abominations (Eze. 7:2). Disaster strikes everywhere because wickedness is universal.

It is more common to find references to the "four winds" or just "winds" in the Bible. In his vision of God's care for Israel, Zechariah saw the four chariots of divine judgment "going forth to the four winds of heaven" after they presented themselves before the Lord. They received the assignment of patrolling the earth (Zech. 6:5). Jeremiah envisions the coming judgment against Jerusalem as "a hot wind from the bare heights in the desert." The wind is not like the cool, refreshing breeze from the west but like the blast of heat from a furnace. It withers the grass and destroys the vegetation (Jer. 4:11, 12). Isaiah referred to the destructive winds of God's wrath when he wrote, "The grass withers, the flower fades, when the breath of the Lord blows upon it" (Isa. 40:7).

Among other terrors of the last days, the prophet Jeremiah visualized a terrible storm like a whirling tempest break upon the head of the wicked. The horrible wind would not cease until God has fully executed His purpose (Jer. 23:19, 20). God's word of judgment is like a blast of heat that causes the "pastures of the shepherds" to mourn, and "the top of Carmel" to wither (Amos 1:2). It is "the east wind, the wind of the Lord" (Hosea 13:15) that the people dread the most because of its devastating impact on the land. The east wind sweeps across the arid desert and sucks up all moisture. But the four winds in the end-time will bring greater terror on the earth's inhabitants. Jeremiah in his oracle of doom against Elam predicted that the impact of God's fierce anger will leave the rulers dead and the land in ruins. The Lord will bring upon the nation the "four winds from the four quarters of heaven" and scatter the Elamites throughout the entire world (Jer. 49:35-38).

During his vision of the four beasts, Daniel saw the four winds of heaven stirring up the sea, after which the four beasts emerged. When God releases the winds, the nations no longer encounter any divine restraint, and they bring destruction and ruin upon the earth (Dan. 7:2-8). The angels in John's vision delay that divinely permitted catastrophe.

"Seventh-day Adventists view the time of terror immediately preceding the sealing of God's saints as a manifestation of the great controversy between Christ and Satan. The destructive forces set in motion when the four winds are released are attributed to Satan. He stirs up nation against nation in an effort to marshal the forces for the last great battle." [1] The angels keep the "armies of Satan at bay" until God completes the sealing of His people. When God finishes it, He will instruct His angels to lift their restraint and allow Satan to "work out his malignity upon the children of disobedience." [2] As the four angels release their control, "all the elements of strife will be let loose. The whole world will be involved in ruin." [3]

The Seal of the Living God (Rev. 7:2-3)   Another angel ascended from the east with the seal of God, and he called to the four angels to hold back the four winds until God's servants were sealed. The reference to the east is more than a picturesque detail. John may have had in mind Ezekiel's vision of the glory of God entering the temple by the east gate. Jesus spoke of the sign of the Son of man appearing in the east (Matt. 24:27, 30). And at the time of His birth, Wise Men from the east came to Palestine in search of the newborn King because of the star they had observed. The fact that the angel with the seal of God arrives from the east, then, indicates good news. Dispatched by God, the angel brings deliverance to the faithful. His summons to the four angels is in behalf of God's people. Before the great tribulation strikes the earth, God will seal, secure, and therefore save His people from destruction.

The seal that the angel bears testified that the faithful belonged to God and were under His authority and power. The picture that John presents goes back to Ezekiel's vision of the marking of the innocent (Eze. 9). In it the Old Testament prophet saw a man clothed in linen with a writing case at his side. The Lord instructed the heavenly messenger to go through the city of Jerusalem and mark the foreheads of those who mourned over the abominations committed in it. When the angel completed his task, God ordered the executioners of the city to smite everyone who did not have the mark in his forehead (Eze. 9:1-7). The sign in the forehead distinguished the faithful from the idolaters and provided them with protection from the judgment awaiting the city.

Some Bible scholars see the picture of sealing in connection with the experience of baptism and the reception of the Holy Spirit. Baptism is a public declaration of a person's consecration to God, and testifies to the fact that he no longer lives for himself but for the Lord. He becomes God's property and possession (Rom. 6). In his letter to the Ephesians Paul wrote, "Do not grieve the Holy Spirit of God, in whom you were sealed for the day of redemption" (Eph. 4:30), an exhortation appearing in the context of his discussion of Christian living. The believers belong to Christ and therefore "must no longer live as the Gentiles do," who in their ignorance and degenerate state of mind are "alienated from the life of God" (Eph. 4:17, 18).

The apostle clearly distinguishes between the believers and the unredeemed. Those who have accepted Christ, being taught "in him, as the truth is in Jesus," have abandoned their old nature, which consisted of greed, licentiousness, deceit, anger, clamor, slander, and malice.

The seal of God has to do with ownership and protection. In his counsel to Timothy concerning false teachers in the church, Paul declared, "God's firm foundation stands, bearing this seal:

'The Lord knows those who are his,' and, 'Let every one who names the name of the Lord depart from iniquity' " (2 Tim. 2:19). While ownership entails protection, it also has its own demands.

The sealing of God's servants in Revelation 7 focuses on the protection that He provides for His people. The assumption is that they have already been tested, have patiently endured the ordeal of suffering, and now await His deliverance. The sealing protects them from the wrath of the divine judgment about to break out against the wicked. The vision answers the question raised at the end of Revelation 6, "Who can stand?" It points to those who bear the seal of the living God.

But to determine what constitutes the seal of the living God, or how one qualifies for this seal, we must go beyond the immediate context. What John does tell us is this: Those who are sealed will not suffer from the events following the release of the four winds. Not until we reach Revelation 14 do we find more information about God's sealed servants. The chapter opens with a vision of the Lamb and the redeemed on Mount Zion. It is a scene of triumph and celebration coming between two solemn appeals for patient endurance in the face of tribulation (Rev. 13:10; 14:12).

The saints of God are clearly the target of the ancient serpent, called the Devil and Satan, the one who deceives the whole world (Rev. 12:9). The serpent is the dragon who gives power to the beast that rises out of the sea to make war against the saints in an effort to conquer them (Rev. 13:7). The context makes clear that we are dealing here with a spiritual conflict, since the main issue involves worship. The eternal destiny of the world's inhabitants centers on a decision to worship the beast and its image, or to worship God, the Creator of heaven and earth (Rev. 14:6-11).

In Revelation 15 we note another scene of victory. John depicts the redeemed standing by the sea of glass in heaven. They hold harps of God and sing the song of Moses and the Lamb. The redeemed can burst forth in their song because they have conquered the beast and its image. Next comes the vision of the seven last plagues that manifest the wrath of God. The angels pour each plague on those who "bore the mark of the beast and worshiped its image" (Rev. 16:2; see Rev. 14:9, 10).

Those who worship the beast and its image receive its imprint in their right hand or in their forehead, signifying that they belong to the evil powers (Rev. 13:16, 17). The mark of the beast entitles them to special economic privileges, sparing them from certain hardships or inconveniences. Out of loyalty to God, however, the saints resist the pressures of the beast and face persecution with patient endurance, pledging their allegiance to God and offering Him their adoration and praise.

The context for understanding the seal of God and for identifying those who bear the seal is the great spiritual conflict during the time of the end. John sees the world separating into two classes of people—those who bear the seal of the living God, and those who wear the mark of the beast. As to what decides who receives the seal and who gets the mark, it is a matter of each person's choice. It centers on whether one chooses to worship God exclusively or whether he seeks through compromise or outright defiance to do obeisance to the beast and its image.

The expression "seal of the living God" warrants closer attention. The book of Revelation contrasts it sharply with the mark of the beast. Unlike the protection and benefits of the beast, which are limited and at best temporary, the protection and blessed state that God provides is everlasting. The "living God" is from everlasting to everlasting, and therefore has the final word. The three angels announcing the hour of God's judgment bear the everlasting gospel (Rev. 14:6). The judgment of God against those who worship the beast and its image will be final and its consequences eternal (Rev. 14:11). The golden bowls that the angels prepare to pour out upon the wicked inhabitants of the earth are full of the wrath of God "who lives for ever and ever" (Rev. 15:7). The message that John wishes to drive home to his readers is clear: God's word of salvation and judgment is the only one to hear, for in the end everyone will have to acknowledge it.

The 144,000 (Rev. 7:4-8) John does not see the actual sealing take place, but hears the number of those involved. We should note two things of interest here: 1. The number itself, 144,000. It makes the most sense when we understand it symbolically. We may arrive at it by multiplying 12 by 12, and then by multiplying that number (144) by 1,000. The number 12 has significance in both the Old and New Testaments. Jacob had 12 sons whose offspring made up the 12 tribes of Israel. Jesus organized His church around the 12 disciples, who became the 12 apostles after His death, and through whom God proclaimed the risen Lord. In his vision of the New Jerusalem John saw the names of the 12 tribes of the sons of Israel inscribed on the 12 gates of the great high wall surrounding the city. He also observed the names of the 12 apostles written on the 12 foundations of the wall of that city (Rev. 21:12-14).

The number 144,000 thus represents the full community of believers, and not a select group separated from a larger body. (One of the Dead Sea scrolls, the Temple scroll, also uses a number to indicate the full community of the righteous, though it is a smaller one, 12,000.) Thus 144,000 indicates completeness or perfection in a sense of a full body of witnesses. The notion of a complete number first appeared in Revelation 6. The vision gives no answer to the martyrs' cry as to how long it would be before God would avenge their blood. Instead, a heavenly source tells them that God will bring judgment upon the earth when the "number of their fellow servants and their brethren should be complete, who were to be killed as they themselves had been" (Rev. 6:10, 11). When the rest of the brethren had perished, the testimony of the martyrs would be finished. The same is true of the 144,000 who will survive the terrors of the last days, and through their patient endurance bear a faithful witness to the world. It is the testimony of the 144,000 at the end of time that constitutes an important part of the great controversy between Christ and Satan. Through their witness God vindicates Himself before the world, and issues His verdict against the evil powers. For that purpose He seals the 144,000.

2. The names of the twelve tribes of Israel. We should not consider it strange to find the remnant numbered among the 12 tribes since we are dealing with symbolic imagery. It was the conviction of the New Testament writers that the followers of Christ constituted the new Israel. Paul called the church "the Israel of God" (Gal. 6:16), reasoning that those who are in Christ are in fact Abraham's seed and therefore rightful heirs of the promises of God (Gal. 3:29). The very titles that Moses ascribes to the Israelites, Peter employs of the church when he refers to them as "a chosen race, a royal priesthood, a holy nation" (1 Peter 2:9). And James apparently addresses the church scattered throughout the Roman world as "the twelve tribes in the Dispersion" (James 1:1). In using such terminology the apostles were consistent with the words of Jesus when He promised the disciples that they would one day appear with Him in the new world and would "sit on twelve thrones, judging the twelve tribes of Israel" (Matt. 19:28).

By enumerating the sealed servants in terms of the 12 tribes of Israel, then, John is simply reiterating a common Christian belief. The church of Jesus Christ is the true Israel of God, the recipients of the blessings that God has in store for His people.

Two things stand out in the list of the 12 tribes. Judah appears before Reuben, the eldest of Jacob's sons (see Gen. 49:3-27). While the order of names is not important (see Deut. 33), there may be a simple explanation for Judah being at the top of the list. The fact that the Messiah came from the tribe of Judah, and that one of the elders referred to the Lamb as "the Lion of the tribe of Judah" (Rev. 5:5) may have led John to place that name before the others. Of more importance is the omission of Dan from the list.

In his final blessing of his sons, Jacob speaks of Dan as "a serpent in the way, a viper by the path, that bites the horse's heels so that his rider falls backward" (Gen. 49:17). According to Jewish tradition, the antichrist would appear among the tribe of Dan and would lead its forces against the people of God.[4]

The Old Testament often connects the tribe of Dan with idolatry. During the period of the tribal confederacy Dan migrated to the north and settled in Laish, where they set up a religious image for themselves (Judges 18:27-31). Later, during the time of the divided monarchy, Jeroboam established an important shrine in Dan as a rival to the Temple in Jerusalem in an effort to strengthen his political influence in the northern kingdom (1 Kings 12:25-30). Given the fact that the great conflict between good and evil focuses on the issue of worship, it is not at all surprising to find the name Dan—one associated with gross idolatry—stricken from the list of the 12 tribes. In its place we find added that of Manasseh (one of Joseph's sons).

---

[1] See *The SDA Bible Commentary,* Ellen G. White Comments, vol. 7, p. 968.

[2] *The SDA Bible Commentary,* vol. 7, p. 781.

[3] White, *The Great Controversy,* p. 614

[4] Barclay, *The Revelation of John,* vol. 2, p. 25.

From Tribulation to Triumph

(Based on Revelation 7:9-17)

"Surely goodness and mercy shall follow me all the days of my life; and I shall dwell in the house of the Lord for ever" (Ps. 23:6).

The Vision of the Great Multitude (Rev. 7:9-12)   Following the sealing of the 144,000, John observed a great multitude of the redeemed. We should note several contrasts between this vision and the previous one on the sealing of the servants of God.

1. Unlike the 144,000, the great multitude cannot be numbered. The sealed servants come from the 12 tribes of Israel, whereas the great multitude consists of the redeemed from all nations, tribes, peoples, and tongues.

2. With the vision of the great multitude the scene shifts from earth to heaven. At the same time we detect a change in mood. The sealing of the servants of God takes place against the dark and grim background of God's impending judgment. The fury of His wrath looms over the wicked like a violent storm. But terror and gloom give way to unrestrained joy as we move from earth to heaven.

Two things stand out in John's description of the great multitude: 1. They wore white robes. The robes symbolize their triumph over evil powers and suggests several things: a. It was a triumph made possible through faith in the Lord Jesus. In His farewell discourse to His disciples on the Mount of Olives, Jesus warned of the persecution that His followers would face. All nations would hate them because of His name. So intense would their suffering be that many would give in to the enemy and abandon the faith. Fellow believers would betray them, but those who endured the tribulation would be saved (Matt. 24:9-13).

b. Triumph came after tribulation. Only sacrifice can produce victory over the forces of wickedness. Those who sought an easy path would fail. Repeatedly, Jesus stressed the need for self-denial. The one who loses his life for Christ's sake will find it in the end (Matt. 16:25). The gate to life is narrow and the way hard

(Matt. 7:14). Recognizing the need for a militant faith, Paul admonished the church to be strong in the Lord and to put on the whole armor of God, for it contended against superhuman powers of wickedness (Eph. 6:10-17). The way to the kingdom will follow the path of suffering because of the evil forces against which we must do battle.

c. The sacrifice of Christ made triumph possible. The white robes symbolize a purity of faith arising from a saving relationship with Jesus. The redeemed washed their robes and made them white in the blood of the Lamb (Rev. 7:14). The sacrifice of Jesus removes the stain of sin, a purging process that empowers the believer and enables him to gain victory over sin. The Christian must fight the battle on two fronts: the war against the evil forces without, and the struggle against sinful tendencies within one's life.

2. The great multitude had palm branches in their hands. The palm branch symbolizes festive joy, usually on the occasion of a military victory. The scene calls to mind the triumphant entry of Christ into Jerusalem. At that time a great crowd took palm branches and went out to meet Him, and as they waved the palm branches, they shouted, "Hosanna! Blessed is he who comes in the name of the Lord" (John 12:13). *Hosanna* is Hebrew for "save us." Joy and a plea for salvation mingled together. In John's vision the celebration anticipates Christ's triumph over the wicked. It may be that the prophet intends to associate the victory of the great multitude with that which Christ achieved at Calvary.

The scene in heaven centers on worship. The praise begins with an exclamation of unrestrained joy from the innumerable saints who represent every nation, kindred, tongue, and people. With a loud cry they exclaim, "Salvation belongs to our God who sits upon the throne, and to the Lamb" (Rev. 7:10). The salvation they refer to has to do with their triumph over the evil powers, their deliverance through the tribulation, and their victory over sin. In every aspect and at every point, only sheer grace can lead to salvation. We may speak of the necessity of faith, the proper exercise of the will, the importance of discipline; we may talk about the need for self-denial and self-sacrifice; and we may emphasize the value of Bible study, prayer, and meditation. But in no way can we attribute our defeat of sin or our triumph over the evil forces of the end-time as a human achievement. From beginning to end, our salvation comes from God's saving grace in

Christ Jesus. Our part is one of choosing. To win with Christ, we decide to follow His instruction, to place our lives in His hands, and to yield our will in absolute submission to the Father. Victory is possible only to the extent that Christ guides our steps, directs our thinking, and influences our judgment. We can hardly, then, call it a human accomplishment!

Following the praise of the great multitude, the entire angelic host "numbering myriads of myriads and thousands of thousands" Rev. 5:11) prostrate themselves before the throne in worship. The angelic doxology consists of a sevenfold ascription of praise introduced and concluded with liturgical "amens."

1. They offer Him blessing. The Greek word is *eulogia*, meaning to speak well. The angelic blessing is more than an outburst of joy and gratitude.

2. They ascribe to Him glory. In the original the word is *doxa*, from which we get our word doxology. To ascribe glory to God, we must be mindful of His majesty and splendor. The angels never become weary of praising God, for they are ever conscious of the radiance emanating from His presence.

3. They attribute to Him wisdom. The Greek *sophia* is the origin of the English word "philosophy." In Eph. 3:9, 10 Paul speaks of God making known His manifold wisdom to the principalities and powers in heavenly places through the church. The plan of redemption reveals God's wisdom to the angels.

4. They offer Him thanksgiving. The original *eucharistia* is the source of the word "Eucharist," the liturgical term for the Lord's Supper. Thanksgiving is their response to the salvation God has provided in Jesus.

5. They give Him honor by their public acknowledgment of His accomplishments in Christ.

6. They ascribe to Him power. In the Greek the word is *dunamis*, from which comes our word "dynamite." It has to do with the ability to preform or accomplish something. God discloses His power through His saving deeds or mighty acts in history. The angels love to sing God's praises for His redemptive work.

7. They praise Him for His might. The Greek word denotes "strength" as evident in God's presence in history. The angels' doxology thus forms an appropriate response to the exclamation of praise from the great multitude.

The Great Tribulation of the Saints (Rev. 7:13, 14)   Our attention shifts from the scene of worship to one of the elders who addresses John with the rhetorical question "Who are these, clothed in white robes, and whence have they come?"

John replies, "Sir, you know." And the elder proceeds to answer his own question. "These are they who have come out of the great tribulation; they have washed their robes and made them white in the blood of the Lamb" (Rev. 7:13, 14).

The question-and-answer format echoes the dialogue between Zechariah and the angel (Zech. 4:2, 4, 5, 11-14; 5:2, 6, 10; 6:4-8) and serves to introduce the explanation of the vision. John's reply to the elder recalls Mary's response to the gardener on Resurrection morning (John 20:15). The word that the RSV translates as "sir" may be seen as an expression of courtesy, and therefore we should not take it as a reference to Jesus.

Two things in the elder's answer deserve our attention: 1. He describes the saints as having come out of "the great tribulation." The use of the definite article in the RSV more accurately translates the Greek text, and suggests that John has in mind the tribulation that Jesus foretold in His discourse on the Mount of Olives (Matt. 24:21; Mark 13:19). Thus it is not trouble in general, but the great terrors at the end of human history, unprecedented in their horror and scope. Such unprecedented turmoil constitutes the final series of woes before the world ends. It is the "time of trouble" prophesied by Daniel (Dan. 12:1), and the "hour of trial which is coming on the whole world" that Christ spoke of in His message to the church in Philadelphia (Rev. 3:10).

The point of the vision, however, is not to dwell on the frightening tribulation. Rather it focuses on the victory achieved. The church will go through the tribulation triumphantly. Awaiting the believers is not the shame of defeat but the glory of conquest.

2. The saints have washed their robes in the blood of the Lamb. The symbol of white robes and soiled garments is common in the Bible. Isaiah compares our righteous deeds to polluted garments (Isa. 64:6), and elsewhere holds out the divine promise of the Lord to cleanse our sinful deeds and make them as white as snow and wool (Isa. 1:18). In a penitential prayer the psalmist pleads with God to wash him thoroughly and to purge him with hyssop (a plant used in religious ceremonies) so that he may be clean (Ps. 51:2, 7, 10).

God instructed Moses to have the people of Israel consecrate themselves and wash their garments in preparation for their appearance before Him (Ex. 19:10). It is an awesome experience to encounter the holiness of God. Zechariah's vision of Joshua the high priest, who stood before the angel of the Lord in filthy garments, presents a similar picture. Satan, the accusing angel, brought charges against him, but the Lord rebuked Satan and defended Joshua as "a brand plucked from the fire." The angel of the Lord immediately ordered those standing by to remove the priest's filthy garments, and then, turning to Joshua, he declared, "Behold, I have taken your iniquity away from you, and I will clothe you with rich apparel" (Zech. 3:1-4).

The saints have made their robes white by washing them in the blood of the Lamb. We must interpret such metaphorical language within the context of the gospel. The merits of Christ's sacrifice are what is of foremost importance. The blood of the Lamb has the purging power that makes the robes white. The saints' act of washing their garments is one of faith in Christ Jesus and not a meritorious work.

This act of faith involves several things: a. The believer makes clear by word and deed his sorrow for sins and his desire to bring about change in his life. b. He accepts the fact of Christ's atoning sacrifice on his behalf, believing that Christ's shed blood frees him from the final penalty of sin. c. He confesses his sins to the Lord and asks for God's forgiveness and cleansing. d. He presents his plans to make amends and to live for Christ before the Lord, and asks for guidance and strength to carry out his intentions. e. He acts on his plans with the full conviction that the Lord has heard his prayer, has removed the sin from his life, and will guide and direct his steps.

The faith that comes from hearing the gospel (Rom. 10:17) consists of sound thinking, firm believing, and decisive action. However, the Christian experiences victory not because he thinks positively or believes optimistically, but because he acts confidently in Christ. And his confidence arises from strong conviction because he not only thinks, or believes, that Christ gives him the victory; he *knows* with certainty!

The saints go through the tribulation successfully because they possess the saving knowledge of the gospel of Christ Jesus. And by acting on it, they appropriate the merits of Christ's sacrifice and thus experience by grace the cleansing power of His blood.

Serving God Day and Night (Rev. 7:15)   Clothed in white robes—the righteousness of Christ—the saints can stand before

God's holy presence and offer Him their consecrated service. Two pictures from the Old Testament come to mind:

1. The scene painted by the psalmist of God's providential care in Psalm 23. After reciting the blessings of God, he speaks of dwelling in the house of God forever (Ps. 23:6). The psalmist has in mind the temple and the special benefits it offers him:

a. The temple was a place of refuge. When Adonijah feared for his life, he fled to the sanctuary and caught hold of the horns of the altar as a plea for mercy (1 Kings 1:49-53). The sanctuary served as a shelter against the avenger. In Psalm 27 David expresses his supreme confidence in the Lord as the stronghold of his life. Evildoers may assail him with their slandering lies, his adversaries may encamp about him preparing for war, but he will remain confident. He will seek after the Lord to dwell in His house and there find shelter in the day of trouble (Ps. 27:1-6).

b. The temple was a place for refreshment. The psalmist writes, "My flesh faints for thee, as in a dry and weary land where no water is. So I have looked upon thee in the sanctuary, beholding thy power and glory" (Ps. 63:1, 2). Deprived of the privilege of attending the temple services, the psalmist mourns. "My tears have been my food day and night, while men say to me continually, 'Where is your God?' " (Ps. 42:3).

c. The temple was a place for celebration. Throughout the Psalter we find exhortations to enter God's presence with thanksgiving (Ps. 95:2), to praise Him among the nations (Ps. 96:3), to come before Him with singing (Ps. 100:2). The psalms abound with such invitations to worship. God enjoys hearing His people sing His praises, for in this way He shares His glory with us. In extolling Him, we participate in His greatness and renew our spirit. That is why it is important for us to acclaim Him continually.

2. The allusion to Israel's exodus from Egypt. The promise that God will shelter His people with His presence brings to mind memories of the pillar of cloud and the pillar of fire that accompanied Israel through the wilderness, and the Shekinah glory that symbolized God in the midst of His people (Ex. 13:21, 22; 40:34-38).

Isaiah envisioned a time when God would wash away the filth of Zion and thoroughly cleanse the city of its sins and re-create His dwelling place. Then a cloud would hover over Mount Zion by day, and smoke and a shining fire by night. They would serve as a canopy and a pavilion to provide shade and shelter for God's people (Isa. 4:4-6). Ezekiel spoke of a time when God would establish His dwelling place in the midst of His people forever. It would be a sign to the nations that God had set Israel apart to be His people and He their God (Eze. 37:27).

The scene of the saints before God's throne, serving Him day and night and enjoying the shelter of His presence, thus depicts the lofty hopes and aspiration of God's people. An appropriate picture following the vision of God's wrath against the wicked and the great tribulation of the saints, it assures the believer that sin will not rise again nor evil to terrify and destroy God's creation.

The Lamb Will Be Their Shepherd (Rev. 7:16, 17) The scene of eternal bliss continues with language and imagery drawn from Old Testament traditions concerning the Messiah and the messianic-age. Revelation 7:16, 17 reflects Isaiah 49:10: "They shall not hunger or thirst, neither scorching wind nor sun shall smite them, for he who has pity on them will lead them, and by springs of water will guide them." Here Isaiah describes the return of the exiles from Babylonian captivity, and in doing so he himself draws from the Exodus traditions of God's care for Israel during their wilderness journey (Ex. 15:22-27; 16:9-12).

John adapts the language and the meaning of the passage by inserting his own words, indicating that the Messianic hopes of Israel have their ultimate fulfillment in Jesus Christ, the Lamb. But he gives an interesting twist: the Lamb will be their shepherd. The metaphor builds on the Old Testament picture of God as the shepherd of Israel (see Ps. 23; Isa. 40:11; Eze. 34:23; 37:24). It also echoes the way Jesus characterized His relationship with His people. He spoke of Himself as the good shepherd who lays down His life for His sheep (John 10:11). In this way the shepherd becomes the sacrificial lamb.

To appreciate the picture John paints for us, it helps to remember what Judea was like during Bible times. Judea consisted largely of a narrow mountain ridge or spine with rugged cliffs and steep ravines leading down to the Dead Sea on the east, and a drop to the low hills of the Shephelah on the west side. In such wild country shepherds had no fences or walls to prevent the sheep from wandering. So the shepherd had to be on constant guard against wild beasts attacking and scattering the flock. It was a difficult job, demanding a great deal of the shepherd. Only the most dedicated ones would endure the inconveniences and hardships of sleepless nights and days of scorching heat. Self-denial and self-sacrifice were the hallmarks of the good shepherd. Perhaps that explains why Jesus compared Himself to one who tends sheep as a way of life.

The Lamb's work as shepherd consists of two things: 1. He guides His flock to springs of living water. To the Palestinian shepherd, the fountain of water in the desert would mean an oasis, a place for the sheep to feed as well as to drink. But the image of such water came to mean much more than mere refreshment. The phrase reminds one of Jesus' words to the Samaritan woman who came to draw water from Jacob's well. The water He offered her would quench her thirst forever. He did not mean that she would never physically drink again, but that the water that He provides becomes a "spring of water welling up to eternal life" (John 4:13, 14).

John provides a similar picture in the concluding vision of the book of Revelation. He depicts the river of the water of life flowing from the throne of God and of the Lamb (Rev. 22:1). Here we note the ultimate source of such living water—the Creator. The Lamb in the midst of the throne guides His flock to the springs of living water that issue from the throne and provide eternal life.

2. He wipes away the tears from every eye. Here we find the fulfillment of Christ's words, "Blessed are those who mourn, for they shall be comforted" (Matt. 5:4). Just as Christ is the only one who can satisfy the spiritual thirst of humankind, He alone can offer lasting comfort. John may have had in mind the prophecy of Isaiah concerning the last days, "He will swallow up death for ever, and the Lord God will wipe away tears from all faces" (Isa. 25:8). In the vision of the New Jerusalem the revelator heard God announce that He was establishing His dwelling place with the redeemed, and that He was abolishing death and dying, sickness and suffering. Humanity will no longer have reason to mourn and cry, and God will wipe every tear from every eye (Rev. 21:3, 4).

The vision of the great multitude ends with this blissful scene. The Great Shepherd provides refreshment, nurture, and lasting comfort for those He redeemed.

God's Church in a Hostile World

(Based on Revelation 8)

"The Lord is in his holy temple; let all the earth keep silence before him" (Hab. 2:20).

The Seventh Seal: Silence in Heaven (Rev. 8:1) Revelation 8 begins with the Lamb opening the seventh seal of the scroll. Then follows a dramatic and ominous silence in heaven, one that becomes all the more conspicuous when considered against the background of the loud and continuous praise of the angels, elders, and four living creatures (Rev. 4:8-11; 5:8-14; 7:10-12). The silence was brief, lasting for approximately half an hour.

Of the different explanations that commentators have advanced, three are important to us because of contextual considerations.

1. The first view associates the silence with the prayers of the saints arising to God mingled with the incense offered by the angel attending the altar (Rev. 8:3, 4).[1] Those holding this position emphasize God's attentiveness to the needs of His people: "Even the music of heaven and even the thunder of revelation are stilled so that God's ear may catch the whispered prayer of the humblest of his trusting people."[2] The prayers of the saints are offered on the altar as a sacrifice to God, and are enveloped in perfumed incense, indicating the sweet and pleasant effect that they have on the Lord.

2. Another interpretation understands the silence to be a dramatic pause to add emphasis to the judgments about to break upon the earth with the sounding of the trumpets.[3] Representatives of this school of thought appeal to the fact that the angel at the golden altar not only mingles the incense with the prayers of the saints, but that he also takes the censer, fills it with fire from the altar, and throws it on the earth. The silence heightens the intensity of the scene, and creates a dreadful expectation of impending doom. This position does not have to exclude the one

who sees the silence as a time when God takes special note of the prayers of His people. Since the judgments as signaled by the trumpets manifest God's wrath, we can understand them as coming in response to the pleas of God's people for relief from the persistent persecution of the enemy.

3. A third explanation sees the silence connected with the second coming of Christ. Heaven is without sound because its hosts have left the celestial courts to accompany Christ.[4] This position has the advantage of encompassing the two views identified above, while broadening the perspective at the same time. The fact that the silence occurs after the breaking of the seventh or last seal makes it even more plausible. At this point, the scroll of destiny containing the mystery of God's holy will may now be revealed. And such a revelation can take place only at the end of time. The Second Advent is the occasion when God will make known the eternal destiny of every human life.

The return of Jesus thus becomes a day of deliverance for some, but a time of terror for others. It brings salvation and judgment to the earth at the same time (see Rev. 6:16, 17). And in this sense we may see the Second Advent as God's response to the prayers of His people. The closing prayer of the book of Revelation testifies to this fact: "Amen. Come, Lord Jesus" (Rev. 22:20).

Three Old Testament texts shed light on the meaning of our passage. a. The message of the prophet Habakkuk. Being a contemporary of Jeremiah, he prophesied just before the Chaldeans invaded his homeland, the country of Judah. The imminent national catastrophe posed a serious problem for the prophet and he addressed it in his book, which consists for the most part of a soliloquy between himself and God.

Deeply disturbed over the increased injustice and violence among his fellow countrymen, he complains to God: "How long shall I cry for help, and thou wilt not hear? Or cry to thee 'Violence!' and thou wilt not save?" (Hab. 1:2). God informs the prophet that He is sending the Chaldeans as a punishment against His people for their social abuse and lawlessness. The thought of God using a more wicked nation (the Chaldeans) to punish a less evil one disturbs Habakkuk even more, and he challenges divine wisdom (verse 13). But God responds and satisfies the prophet. In humble submission Habakkuk states, "The Lord is in his holy temple; let all the earth keep silence before him" (Hab. 2:20).

The silence that he admonished the earth to observe originates from an intense expectation of coming judgment (Hab. 3:3-15)—a judgment that brings doom to the wicked while offering salvation to God's people. During such a time of terror, "the righteous shall live by his faith" (Hab. 2:4). The coming of the Lord, moreover, will be a glorious manifestation of His power that evokes from His people an exclamation of praise (Hab. 3:3, 18).

b. The admonition of Zechariah. In a message of hope to the Jewish people, the prophet points to the future when God will first judge the nations that have plundered Judah and Jerusalem, and then will establish His dwelling in the midst of His people, offering them comfort and restoring their prosperity. The prophecy concludes with a sober command: "Be silent, all flesh, before the Lord; for he has roused himself from his holy dwelling" (Zech. 2:13). Again we find silence clearly associated with the coming of the Lord. An awareness of the imminent event leaves everyone in a state of wonder as to the significance and the consequence of His appearance.

c. The prophecy of Zephaniah. Zephaniah was the last of the minor prophets who foretold of the coming judgment against the nation of Judah. Central to his book's message is the prophet's interest in the "day of the Lord." Looking beyond the immediate horizon of the approaching doom, he directs our attention to the terrors at the end-time when the wrath of God will be revealed to all the earth's wicked inhabitants. The great day of the Lord will be an occasion of distress and anguish, one of ruin and devastation, darkness and gloom (Zeph. 1:14-16). In that day the fire of God's jealous wrath will consume the entire earth, bringing all its inhabitants to a sudden end (verse 18). This ominous view leads the prophet to issue a sobering summons: "Be silent before the Lord! For the day of the Lord is at hand" (verse 7).

In each passage the respective prophet exhorts the earth's inhabitants to keep silence in view of the coming judgment. The anticipation of God's imminent action dominates the scene and forms the basis for the prophetic appeal. The Lord prepares to leave His holy dwelling to visit the earth, and His arrival will drive the wicked into dreadful despair. John takes the themes of silence, judgment, and the Lord's coming, and forms his own picture based on the vision in heaven. Instead of focusing on the earth, however, the revelator pictures what heaven will be like when God leaves His holy dwelling and heads for earth. Absolute silence results, for the entire heavenly throng accompanies the

Lord. All heaven attends the event of the second advent of Christ.

The Prayers of the Saints (Rev. 8:3-5)   Immediately pre-ceding the return of Jesus, God's people will endure the great tribulation that Christ spoke of in His farewell discourse to His disciples (Matt. 24:15-31). It is a time when God seems to be silent: "To human sight it will appear that the people of God must soon seal their testimony with their blood as did the martyrs before them. They themselves begin to fear that the Lord has left them to fall by the hand of their enemies. It is a time of fearful agony. Day and night they cry unto God for deliverance." [5] Here we encounter the prayers of the saints that the angel attending the golden altar before the throne mingles with the perfumed incense.

God is the great rescuer of His people, and He will not ignore their pleas for intervention. Their faith has been perfected through their patient endurance in accordance with God's plan. He will save them by offering not escape but conquest. The Lord promises to deliver us *through* the temptation, not *from* it. Because of the insidious nature of sin, God seeks to develop His character in us in the midst of affliction because that is when our hearts are most receptive to His Spirit. It is during times of sorrow and intense grief that we most often turn to the Lord for comfort and emotional renewal. Sad times have a way of opening our souls to God, allowing Him to heal our wounds and strengthen our spirit. The Lord wants to develop characters in His people that will enable them to endure any kind of trouble and distress, and through it all remain upright, full of courage and confidence. For God delights to take His people from tragedy to triumph, and from shame to glory.

The prayers of the saints thus arise out of their sheer need of God's redemptive grace. But the prayers also express trust in His faithfulness. Their confidence enables them to persevere in prayer night and day because they share the conviction so well stated by the psalmist: "Our God comes, he does not keep silence, before him is a devouring fire, round about him a mighty tempest" (Ps. 50:3).

Examining John's vision of the angel at the golden altar, we note two things: 1. The work of intercession. The presiding angel does not make the prayers of the saints acceptable to God but simply presents them before God. His ministry serves to enhance the significance that God attaches to the prayers of His people and the interest that God's angels have in their spiritual needs.

When the angel added incense to the hot coals on the altar, a cloud of fragrant smoke arose that signified divine acceptance. The scene brings to mind Paul's statement in his letter to the Ephesians that Christ's death on the cross was a loving act on their behalf and a fragrant offering and sacrifice to God (Eph. 5:2). John's vision of heaven suggests that the fervent prayers of God's people have sacrificial value. By way of the altar, the saints and their prayers enter into God's presence.

2. The work of judgment. The prophet saw the angel take the golden censer used to mingle the incense with the prayers of the saints, and fill it with fire from the altar. Then he threw it on the earth. "Peals of thunder, voices, flashes of lightning, and an earthquake" followed (Rev. 8:5), indicating that God was about to respond to those prayers. We may see in this response an answer in part to the martyrs' plea for vengeance (Rev. 6:10). The symbolic act of the attending angel reminds us of Ezekiel's vision of the man clothed in linen, who, upon receiving divine instruction, filled his hands with burning coals from between the cherubim, and scattered them over the city of Jerusalem. The ritual indicated the divine judgment about to fall upon the city because of the abominations committed in it (Eze. 10:1, 2).

The fire from the censer brings new terrors upon the earth, a manifestation of divine wrath that comes in answer to the prayers of the saints. The prayers do not express a lust for revenge but a plea for deliverance. The vengeance is God's response to the suffering of His people. His wrath kindles against the wicked, and breaks upon them like a devouring fire that burns until it consumes everything.

The First Four Trumpets (Rev. 8:2, 6-12)   The world of the Old Testament employed trumpets for a variety of purposes, one of which was to sound the alarm in time of war. We may understand the seven trumpets in John's vision best against such a background. John observed the seven angels standing before God's throne receive seven trumpets. Their mission was to announce a new series of woes that God prepared to send upon the earth and its inhabitants. The blowing of the trumpets may represent three things:

1. God's warning message to the world. The events that take place with the blasting of the trumpets are not natural disasters even though they may be catastrophes in nature. The Bible writers attribute such calamities to God, and see them as manifestations of His displeasure and wrath. We misunderstand

and misinterpret the biblical message when we try to explain the events as arising from natural causes. The fact is that we will not find a scientific basis for connecting natural events to divine judgments. And we do not need to do so. Instead, we need only to see God's hand at work and discern His ultimate intent in such events. In John's vision of the seven trumpets, the disasters reveal God's anger against the enemies of His church for their vicious assaults and blasphemous rebellion. They constitute a divine warning that time for repentance is rapidly running out.

2. God's summons to His church. The trumpets not only warn the unrepentant of impending danger but also call God's people to prepare for war in the concluding phase of the great conflict between good and evil. The best defense against evil is the offensive fight of faith. The militant church will become the triumphant church in the end-time, for the preparations we make to do battle with the enemy keep us spiritually sensitive to our need of God's resources.

3. God's announcement of His coming. At the time of the Second Advent, Christ will send out His angels with the sound of a trumpet blast, and they will gather the redeemed from one end of heaven to another (Matt. 24:31). Paul tells the Thessalonians that the Lord will descend from heaven "with a cry of command, with the archangel's call, and with the sound of the trumpet of God" (1 Thess. 4:16).

The seven trumpets in John's vision thus serve these three basic functions. With each trumpet blast, we find the forces of nature hurled against a part of the world. The destruction is terrible but limited, since God's judgment is not yet final. He does not intend it to be retributive but to lead human beings to repentance. The trumpets appear in three sequences, the first four directed against the natural world and separated from the fifth and sixth trumpets (Rev. 9:1-21) by the eagle's announcement of the three woes (Rev. 8:13). The seventh trumpet appears in Revelation 11, following an interlude (Rev. 10:1-11; 11:1-14). With each sequence, the divine judgments become more severe as the conflict between good and evil intensifies.

1. *The First Trumpet: Hail, Fire, and Blood* (Rev. 8:7). When the first angel sounds his trumpet, hail and fire mixed with blood fall upon the earth. Once again we note the impact of the Old Testament on John's thought and imagery. The plagues of Egypt during the time of Moses provide his main source of allusions. Specifically, it was the seventh plague that rained hail upon the

land (Ex. 9:13-35). The plague devastated the entire country, striking down everything in the open field—man, beast, tree, and plant—whereas the destruction that followed the blast of the first trumpet scorched a third part of the earth, trees, and grass. The judgment signaled by the trumpet was not intended to be final but a warning to the earth's inhabitants to repent.

2. *The Second Trumpet: The Sea Becomes Blood* (Rev. 8:8, 9). The blast of the second trumpet affects the sea and its creatures and ships. John sees a great mountain on fire cast from heaven into the sea, turning the latter into blood and leaving one third of the sea creatures dead and one third of the ships destroyed. Some see in the destruction an allusion to volcanic activity in the Aegean, but such an explanation fails to note the purpose of the vision. The natural phenomena that the revelator describes serve to reveal the judgments of God against a rebellious world. John does not start with a natural event and move toward a religious explanation. Rather he understands the phenomena as arising from a divine intervention to warn and lead earth's inhabitants to repentance. The judgment parallels the first plague of Egypt that transformed the rivers into blood, killing the fish and making the water undrinkable (Ex. 7:20, 21). The judgment from the second trumpet affected the world food supply and commerce.

3. *The Third Trumpet: The Falling Star* (Rev. 8:10, 11). When the third angel blew his trumpet, John observed a great star plummet from heaven, blazing like a torch. It fell on the fresh water and turned a third part of it into wormwood. The water became bitter and was lethal to those who drank it. Like the lightning storm and burning mountain, the meteorite symbolizes the divine visitation to warn the world of the wrath to come upon the unrepentant. The contamination of the fresh water supply reminds us of the first plague of Egypt, which transformed the water into blood.

The name of the falling star is Wormwood, suggesting two things. a. The judgment would leave a bitter effect on the earth's inhabitants. Wormwood is the name of a plant with an unpleasant taste. While the plant is not poisonous, it can make a person quite sick. b. Also wormwood symbolizes bitterness and sorrow, and the Old Testament associates the word with Israel's idolatrous ways (Deut. 29:17, 18; Amos 6:12; Jer. 9:14, 15).

4. *The Fourth Trumpet: The Darkening of the Sun, Moon, and Stars* (Rev. 8:12). When the fourth angel blasted forth his trumpet, one third of the luminaries darkened. The prophet does not state

the actual effect on the earth's inhabitants except that a third of the day passed in total darkness, and a third part of the night as well. The judgment corresponds to the ninth plague against Egypt that lasted for three days. Some see in the allusion to the plagues of Egypt an effort to associate God's deliverance to His people in the last days with His rescue of the Hebrew slaves from Egyptian bondage. In this respect, the exodus from Egypt would be a type of the exodus from a hostile world to the Promised Land in the world to come.

Throughout the Old Testament we find references to darkness as a sign of divine judgment. In his message of doom against the kingdom of Israel, Amos told the people that the day of the Lord would be one of darkness and not of light. Instead of bringing deliverance to God's people as was usually the case, it would result in destruction (Amos 5:19). The prophet Joel in a similar way spoke of the day of the Lord as an occasion of darkness and gloom, since it would be the time when God would visit His people with judgment. The thick darkness on the earth for one third of the day and one third of the night symbolizes, however, God's judgment upon the unbelieving, unrepentant world and not upon the church or the faithful. Since John's vision has to do with the end of human history, the only classes of people then in existence will be the faithful and the faithless.

The New Testament also employs the symbols of light and darkness when describing the conflict between good and evil. Darkness is the sphere of the evil powers, who prey on the earth's inhabitants through deceit and error. The demons who dwell in darkness cannot withstand the light. When the light shines, the darkness cannot overcome it, so there is in fact no contest between the two (John 1:5, 9). God's judgment against the world centers around their preference for sin (John 3:19-21). The darkness that comes with the blast of the fourth trumpet represents God's turning away from the wicked. It is a prelude to their final rejection at the end, when the inhabitants of the earth will have placed themselves under Satan's full control, "the deceiver of the whole world" (Rev. 12:9; 20:7, 8).

The Eagle's Warning (Rev. 8:13)   After the fourth trumpet and the judgment associated with it, John heard an eagle cry with a loud voice as it flew in midheaven. Its scream announced doom in the form of three woes that would follow the blasts of the remaining three trumpets. The picture of a solitary eagle flying in midheaven breaks the sequence of the trumpets and serves to dramatize and intensify the judgment message to come. It does so in two ways: 1. The eagle has a reputation for its strength and swiftness. Its symbolic usage at this point suggests that the doom to follow will be quick and devastating. 2. As a bird of prey, its presence in midheaven indicates the impending danger of the earth's inhabitants and adds emphasis to the divine warning implicit in the trumpet blasts. We may also see it as an ominous forecast of the "great supper of God" when heaven summons the birds of prey to eat the flesh of the wicked (Rev. 19:17, 18).

[1] William Barclay, *The Revelation of John*, vol. 2, p. 40.

[2] *Ibid.*

[3] Mounce, in *The Book of Revelation*, p. 179.

[4] *The SDA Bible Commentary*, vol. 7, p. 787.

[5] White, *The Great Controversy*, p. 630.

Doom From the Bottomless Pit

(Based on Revelation 9)

"*God is our refuge and strength, a very present help in trouble*" *(Ps. 46:1).*

The Fifth Trumpet: The Bottomless Pit (Rev. 9:1)   With the fifth trumpet the judgment of the pagan world intensifies. We now move from messages of warning to ones of woe. The first four trumpets announced disasters in the world of nature, but the fifth and sixth trumpets bring upon the world the terrors of demonic assault. The first of the demonic woes takes place when the fifth angel blows his trumpet. Following the trumpet blast, John witnesses a star fallen from heaven. The star is a person and therefore differed from the molten mass that John had observed crashing when the third trumpet sounded. This person receives the key to the shaft of the bottomless pit, our first reference to the great abyss in the book of Revelation. Elsewhere the abyss appears in Revelation 9:2, 11; 11:7; 20:1, 3. The image envisions a prison house that confines the fallen angels, the demons, the beast, the false prophet, and Satan himself until the day of their final punishment in the lake of fire (Rev. 20:10, 14, 15).

The abyss or bottomless pit is the antithesis of the court of heaven, just as hell is the opposite of heaven. It represents the headquarters of the evil forces. The fact that Scripture also depicts it as a prison house clearly indicates that the evil powers do not enjoy independence but remain under God's control. The conflict between good and evil takes place only because He allows the rebellious forces to do their work in order to serve His redemptive purpose. It is part of God's character to give everyone an opportunity to present his case, to make his point, and to reveal his own intentions through his course of action.

The book of Isaiah contains a picture of the abyss similar to what we find in the book of Revelation. In a prophecy concerning the judgment and final punishment of the evil forces, the writer tells of God gathering together the hosts of heaven and the kings of the earth and shutting them up in a prison for a period of time, after which He will execute their punishment. The prison house represents the period between their condemnation and final punishment. It serves to restrain them for a limited time (Isa. 24:21, 22).

The sounding of the fifth trumpet thus signals the release of the demonic powers. The terrors that they inflict upon the earth do have restrictions, however (Rev. 9:4). In a strange way, God uses them as instruments of His wrath against the recalcitrant, pagan world (verses 20, 21). This testifies to His absolute sovereignty in the universe. Throughout the controversy God remains in control. Whatever havoc the evil powers bring upon the world, they do so only because He permits it.

The Opening of the Bottomless Pit. (Rev. 9:2-12)   John sees the being with the key to the bottomless pit unlock the shaft, and when he opens it, smoke resembling the smoldering cloud of a great furnace rises to the sky and hovers above the earth so as to darken the sun and the surrounding atmosphere. The smoke billowing from the abyss reminds one of the scene on Mount Sinai at the time of the revelation of the law. The mountain appears to be wrapped in smoke because of the fiery descent of God, for the holiness of God is a consuming fire. The smoke at Sinai is simply the earth's response to His presence. The smoke continues to rise as the trumpet blast grows louder and louder (Ex. 19:18, 19). In the vision of Revelation, John regards the smoke streaming from the abyss as a response to the trumpet blast, announcing God's judgment.

After the smoke, locusts emerge. John's elaborate description of the creatures falls into two parts. Having identified their origin, he proceeds to define their mission. Essentially it consists in their inflicting torture on the unredeemed portion of humanity (Rev. 9:4). We note several things about their power and authority:

1. It is limited. What power they have God has given to them, indicating once again that the evil forces do not and cannot function apart from His permission. From the very beginning of the controversy, they have been under His sovereign control.

2. It is like that of scorpions. Scorpions are slow, nocturnal creatures of the desert. By day they hide under stones or in the crevices and cracks of a wall. When night falls, they crawl from their shelter in search of insects or other small animals. Although scorpions prey mainly on insects, people fear them because of the poisonous sting in their tails. It is seldom fatal to humans, but

it can be extremely painful. As part of His instruction to the 70 disciples, Jesus informed them that He had given them "authority to tread upon serpents and scorpions, and over all the power of the enemy," thus assuring them that nothing would harm them (Luke 10:19). The locusts from the bottomless pit have the power but not the appearance of the scorpion. They are released to inflict injury on the wicked only (Rev. 9:4).

3. It is a power bound by specific restrictions. They have express warnings not to harm the vegetation but to focus their attacks on those who do not have the seal of God upon their foreheads. During the plague against Egypt the swarming locusts devastated the land (Ex. 10:15). The prophet Joel describes the impact of the judgment-plague as one similar to that of a devouring fire: "The land is like the garden of Eden before them, but after them a desolate wilderness, and nothing escapes them" (Joel 2:3). The saints escape the terror miraculously while the rest of the world suffers from the demonic assault.

4. It is a temporary power. God permitts them to torture the wicked for five months, but the locusts cannot kill them. The life cycle of a locust from birth, through the larva stage, to death is five months, a fact that may be the origin of the limited time period. The torture advanced against the earth's inhabitants thus lasts through one generation of locusts. Moreover, the dry season in Palestine is approximately a five-month period (from spring to late summer),[1] the time of year when a locust invasion is most likely to occur. While the permission to torment is temporary, the torture is nevertheless intense. So excruciating is the pain that the victims seek death in an effort to find relief, but death evades them (Rev. 9:5, 6). Here we note an allusion to Jeremiah's Temple sermon in which he foretold of the time when the idolatrous and immoral inhabitants of Judah would prefer death to life (Jer. 8:3).

Having dealt with the origin and mission of the demonic locusts, John next describes their appearance. Their ghastly and grotesque features vividly portray their diabolical nature: 1. They appear like horses arrayed for battle (Rev. 9:7). John seems to be drawing his description from the prophecy of Joel. In Joel's account the swarming locusts sound like the noise of chariots in battle (Joel 2:5). 2. On their heads they wear what look like crowns of gold. Whether in fact or appearance, the locusts are triumphant, or possess the power to complete their mission successfully. 3. Their faces are human, indicating an intelligence superior to that of the insect itself and making them all the more capable of inflicting torture upon their victims. 4. They have hair like women and teeth like those of a lion (Rev. 9:8). The reference to women's hair is not clear. As to the teeth of lions, we note a similar description in Joel's prophecy of the locust plague (Joel 1:6). It may well be that the hair and teeth are simply for effect. Since the locusts do not consume the vegetation, and use their scorpion-like tails to inflict injury, the teeth would emphasize their fierce appearance. 5. The creatures have scales like iron breastplates (Rev. 9:9). The scaly exterior of the locust appears like a coat of armor that protect their bodies from the weapons of their enemies. The noise of their wings in flight sound like the rumbling of horses and chariots rushing into battle. Once again we note imagery drawn from the book of Joel (Joel 2:4, 5). 6. Each locust has a tail like that of a scorpion. The demonic locusts terrify their victims by their appearance and torment them by their sting (Rev. 9:10). Their power to punish is both psychological and physical, affecting both the mind and the body of their victims.

The prophet brings his description of the locust assault to a close with a reference to their king, who has three titles: 1. He is the angel of the bottomless pit. However, he is not the same angel who unlocks the pit, but more like the one responsible for organizing the forces in preparation for battle.[2] 2. His name in Hebrew is *Abaddon*. The title denotes destruction, an appropriate description of the ruler of the demonic locusts. 3. And his name in Greek is *Apollyon*, a designation more accurately rendered "Destroyer."

John concludes his discussion of the events associated with the fifth trumpet with a somber reminder: "The first woe has passed; behold, two woes are still to come" (Rev. 9:12).

The Sixth Trumpet: The Four Angels Released (Rev. 9:13-21) When the sixth angel uses his trumpet, John hears a voice from the golden altar before God. Scripture does not identify the speaker, but we have reason to believe that the command coming from the altar is consistent with the cry for vengeance implicit in the prayers of the saints, and expressed more directly in the plea of the martyrs (Rev. 8:3-5; 6:10). Once again we find ourselves reminded of the importance God attaches to the prayers of His people.

The celestial charge orders the sixth angel to "Release the four angels who are bound at the great river Euphrates" (Rev. 9:13-14). It is the first and only instance when one of the trumpet-angels participates in the event announced by his trumpet blast. The command intensifies the drama. As to the identity of the four angels at the Euphrates, we can only speculate. Unlike the four angels at the four corners of the earth, they are bound at the river. While the four angels hold back the winds of destruction, the angels at the Euphrates bring about destruction upon their release (see Rev. 7:1-3). They appear to have control of the innumerable horde of demonic troops (Rev. 9:15, 16).

The Euphrates River has significance for several reasons: 1. It is one of the four rivers named in the Garden of Eden. 2. In His covenant to Abraham, God promised to give Abraham's descendants the land from the river of Egypt in the Sinai peninsula to the river Euphrates. The divine promise received fulfillment during David's reign in Jerusalem, but after the monarchy the nation divided and the Jewish people had difficulty maintaining those boundaries. The river Euphrates thus stood for the boundary that separated God's people from their enemies. 3. The release of the four angels at the river Euphrates suggests that they represent evil forces organized against God's people. But their freeing does not result in an assault against the saints.

God unleashes them to carry out His judgment upon the pagan world. While the judgment is not final, nevertheless it is quite severe. They are to kill one third of the earth's population. The horror of the last days increases as we move from the fifth trumpet to the sixth one. Whereas the demonic locusts had permission to injure but not destroy, the demonic horsemen have freedom to conduct a widespread massacre (Rev. 9:15).

John continues his description of the army of horsemen by noting their breastplates. Their armor has the color of fire, of sapphire, and of sulphur, the very substances that John saw issuing from the mouths of the horses. Moreover, the horses have heads like those of lions (verse 17). The horror mounts with this grotesque and revolting description. The riders appear to be incidental in the actual execution. The fire-breathing monsters occupy center stage in this drama of destruction. The power of the demonic beasts appears in their tails as well as in their mouths. The picture of cruel torment emerges with this last detail: the victims apparently are wounded by the tail and then scorched by the flaming breaths emanating from the horses' mouths (verses 18, 19).

The picture of the demonic cavalry resembles the description of cruelty and destruction Habakkuk portrays when he envisions the advance of the Chaldean forces into Judah. John also may be drawing his imagery from the description of Leviathan, the sea monster in the book of Job (see Job 41:19-21). The wholesale slaughter committed by the demonic beasts, he says, results from three plagues—fire, smoke, and sulphur. Ironically, they are the materials that God uses to exterminate the devil and his evil cohorts. In the end the lake of fire that burns with sulphur (Rev. 20:10, 14, 15) will consume them.

John brings his presentation of the sixth trumpet to a close with a stunning observation: "The rest of mankind, who were not killed by these plagues, did not repent" (Rev. 9:20). He emphasizes his point by repeating it in the following verse, "Nor did they repent of their murders or their sorceries or their immorality or their thefts." From this astonishing fact we suggest the following conclusions:

1. The divine intention behind the judgment is not to lead the wicked to repentance, but to avenge God's name. The earlier judgments following the blasts of the first four trumpets sought to warn earth's rebellious inhabitants. With the blasting of the fifth and sixth trumpets, however, we move from messages of warning to announcements of woes. To suggest that God summons the demonic forces to torment and terrify the wicked so as to get them to submit constitutes an assault against His character. Instead, we should understand God's action against them as a result of His abandonment of them, thus allowing them to reap the consequences of their persistent course of sin.

2. The phrase "the rest of mankind" refers to the wicked who survive the assault of the demonic cavalry. Since one third of the wicked population perish, we may assume that those remaining constituted two thirds of the people. The figures do not include the people of God. While John does not mention them in the sixth seal, we may conclude that God has protected them against the "three plagues" because of the seal of God upon their foreheads (see Rev. 9:4).

3. John's concluding observation tells us something about sin's horribleness. Despite the fact that the wicked fall prey to the demonic forces, suffering torment and terrible death, those who are spared still refuse to alter their course. Here is an example of demon possession. The victims are helpless and their situation is hopeless. The prophet's description of their sins consists of a sevenfold indictment: a. They manufactured sin. The phrase "the

works of their hands" suggests that they earned their living making idols. They profited from the sins of others, and were doubtlessly encouraging them to sin by promoting their products.

b. They worshiped demons. The depth to which they allowed themselves to plunge was appalling. Not only did they commit sin, but they offered their adoration and praise to the devilish fiends themselves! The pagans enjoyed sinning, took delight in their wickedness, found great pleasure in doing evil, and relished the thought of encouraging others in sin.

c. They worshiped idols of gold, silver, bronze, stone, wood, which could not see, hear, or walk. While there may be no reason to the order in which John lists the materials, we do note that they appear in a sequence of diminishing value. The idol makers manufactured products that met the needs and satisfied the tastes of their customers, creating idols or images for rich and poor and middle-income families. But regardless of the price or the value of the material and workmanship, the idols themselves were not worthy of worship. They could not see the needs of their devotees, or hear their prayers, or act on their behalf.

d. They committed murder. John separates the last four offenses from the previous ones by his repeated comment that the wicked did not repent. We are to understand that evil humanity feels no remorse for the murders it has committed. No hope exists for them. Given the opportunity and the incentive, they will murder again.

e. They practiced sorcery. The Greek term is *pharmakeus*, from which we derive the word "pharmacy." Those who practiced witchcraft made use of chemical potions, which enabled them to impress their clients and exercise power over them. The Bible classifies sorcery as one of the most vile sins (Gal. 5:20), and those who persist in practicing the pagan art are assured a place in the lake of fire (Rev. 21:8). The sorcerers refused to repent despite the horrors God spared them to witness.

f. They lived immorally. In the original the word is "fornication." The sin covers a range of licentious practices that degraded the participants. Owing to the offensive nature of this human abuse, we find this sin listed among those most severely denounced (Rev. 22:15).

g. They mastered the art of thievery. Those who pursue sin become more clever in designing and devising ways to defraud, swindle, and embezzle. When caught, they may express regret for their mistakes, but once released, they resume their dishonesty with greater zeal and delight.

Murder, sorcery, fornication, and theft are intricately bound to idolatry, and constitute the fruit of demon worship when they become a way of life. In his sevenfold list of offenses, John does not refer to an occasional mistake, but a persistent trend, a lifestyle unaltered by the misfortunes of cohorts or the judgments of God. Consequently, there is no way to end the dehumanizing and degrading practices except to cast the offenders in the lake of fire prepared for the devil and his angels (Matt. 25:41).

---

[1] Barclay, *The Revelation of John*, vol. 2, p. 51.
[2] *The SDA Bible Commentary*, vol. 7, p. 792.

The Testing Time

(Based on Revelation 10)

"If it seem slow, wait for it; it will surely come, it will not delay" *(Hab. 2:3).*

The Mighty Angel and the Little Scroll (Rev. 10:1, 2)   Our attention shifts once again to another vision. In the vision of the seven seals John inserts an interlude of two other ones—the sealing of the servants of God, and the great multitude before God's throne—between the sixth and seventh seals. We note the same pattern with the vision of the seven trumpets. An interlude of two visions—the angel with the little scroll, and the two witnesses—appears between the sixth and seventh trumpets. As we study this section we do well to remember that John is not following a chronological sequence, but introducing and arranging his material in a dramatic way so as to drive home basic truths about the struggle between good and evil. He writes to the church in an effort to awaken and nurture hope in the ultimate triumph of God's people during the last days. Faith in the Word of God and the testimony of Jesus will enable them to ride out the storm of controversy with patient endurance.

In vision John sees another angel whose appearance is so distinct as to make it an outstanding feature of the vision. The prophet's description of the angel has led some commentators to conclude that he is the risen Lord Himself.[1] We do note the following facts:

1. He is a mighty angel. John in the vision of the Lamb before God's throne refers to the angel who issued the challenge as a "strong angel" (Rev. 5:2). Revelation 12:7 speaks of "Michael and his angels fighting against the dragon . . . and his angels." And again the prophet distinguishes the angel in Revelation 18 from other angels by calling attention to his great authority and the splendor of his presence (verse 1). While it is infrequent, then, it is not exceptional for John to single out certain angels. But his purpose in doing so is to emphasize the message associated with

their appearance and not to call attention to their personal qualities. In the introductory vision of the risen Lord, however, the message is bound up with Christ's personage.

2. He is wrapped in a cloud. John sees the angel descending from heaven to earth enveloped in a cloud. The picture reminds us of Daniel's vision of the Son of man, who came with the clouds of heaven to present himself before the Ancient of Days (Dan. 7:13). The biblical passages treating the Second Advent speak of Christ arriving "on the clouds of heaven" (Matt. 24:30) or "in clouds with great power and glory" (Mark 13:26). Paul describes the saints as being caught up "in the clouds to meet the Lord" (1 Thess. 4:17).

In the Bible, clouds often symbolize the divine presence (Ex. 13:21, 22). The picture of the angel wrapped in a cloud, then, may indicate a divine manifestation, or that the messenger comes to John directly from the presence of God and the risen Lord.[2] Scripture also sometimes describes clouds as the chariots of God (see Ps. 104:3).

3. A rainbow appears over his head. Here we observe a striking similarity to Ezekiel's description of the Lord enthroned in heaven. In fact, we note that Ezekiel's vision of the Lord mentions the rainbow as it appears in the cloud on the day of rain. Instead of the rainbow hovering over the Lord's head, we find it around the throne. Brightness emanates from the divine presence, His loins and legs appearing like burning fire (Eze. 1:26-28). John's vision of God enthroned also contains a rainbow (it looked like an emerald) circling the throne (Rev. 4:3). The rainbow is a sign of the covenant that God made with Noah, namely, that He would never again destroy the earth by a flood of waters (Gen. 9:13). While John's vision of the mighty angel does not seem to contain any allusion to that divine promise, the fact that the rainbow appears above the angel's head suggests an implicit message of assurance. Following the vision of the sixth trumpet and the terrors associated with it, the rainbow reminds the believer of God's deliverance of the faithful at a time of terrifying destruction and thus offers consolation. God will protect His people in the last days from the storm and fury of His wrath, just as He cared for His people during the terrible times of the Flood period.

4. His face is like the sun. The introductory vision of the risen Lord describes Christ's face similarly. It is "like the sun shining in full strength" (Rev. 1:16). The imagery recalls the experience of

Moses on Mount Sinai with God. He urged God to reveal His glory to him, but the Lord told him that no one could see His face and live; the experience would consume him. So God shielded Moses in a cleft of a rock, covered his face, and allowed the Israelite leader to see only His back (Ex. 33:18-23). After Moses came down from Mount Sinai, the skin of his face so reflected the brilliance of God's glory that he had to veil his face before the people (Ex. 34:29-35). When the risen Lord appeared to Saul of Tarsus on the road to Damascus, He manifested Himself as a magnificent light that dazzled the pharisee, forcing him to his knees in humble submission and leaving him blind and broken in spirit (Acts 9:1-9).

John may well have still another passage in mind when he describes the illustrious appearance of the mighty angel. In the account of Christ's transfiguration, the evangelist states that the face of Jesus "shone like the sun" (Matt. 17:2). Peter, James, and John miraculously envisioned the divine presence in the earthly Jesus, and His majestic splendor overwhelmed them. The radiance emanating from the face of the mighty angel, then, may be a reflection of God's glory or the manifestation of God's presence itself.

5. His legs resemble fire (see Eze. 1:27). The expression "appearance of fire" is a conspicuous allusion to the divine presence in Israel's midst during their wilderness wanderings (Ex. 13:21, 22; 14:24). As mentioned earlier, John may also have in mind the vision of Ezekiel where the prophet describes the loins and the legs of the Lord as "gleaming bronze, like the appearance of fire enclosed round about" (Eze. 1:27). The pillar of fire that went before Israel at night provided guidance and protection. The cloud that appeared during the day provided the same function. We note that John's description of the mighty angel includes both the cloud and the pillar of fire. It may well be that his insertion of the vision at this time seeks to emphasize that God will guide and protect His people during the time of trouble. They can have assurance that they will survive the great tribulation and safely travel to the Promised Land.

6. He has in his hand a little scroll. Unlike the seven-sealed scroll, the little scroll lies open in the angel's hand, an obvious allusion to Ezekiel's vision of the scroll in which the angel spread the parchment out before him and commanded him to eat it. The document contained words of lamentation and mourning, but upon eating it, the Old Testament prophet discovered that it

was "as sweet as honey" in his mouth (Eze. 2:8-3:3). The consuming of the scroll symbolized the prophet's receiving of his commission to proclaim the divine message to his fellow countrymen (Eze. 3:4-11). We find similar instruction in the vision of John. As in the case of Ezekiel, an angel tells him to chew and swallow the scroll, and in doing so he discovers that it is "sweet as honey" in his mouth but bitter in his stomach. And as in Ezekiel's experience, John receives a commission to prophesy (Rev. 10:9-11).

7. His right foot stands on the sea and his left foot on land. The imagery serves to dramatize the angel's awesome appearance by giving magnitude to his presence. By contrast, the little scroll in the angel's hand adds further emphasis to his colossal stature. His imposing figure, moreover, symbolizes his sovereignty over sea and land, and denotes the power and authority from which he issues his declarations and commands (verses 4-11).

The Angel's Message (Rev. 10:3-7)   John hears the mighty angel call "with a loud voice," one commensurate with his enormous size. The prophet tells us four things about the angel's message: 1. He speaks like a roaring lion. Amos depicts God's voice as a roar in his introduction to the oracles of doom against the foreign nations (Amos 1:2) and against Israel (Amos 3:8). In a prophecy concerning Israel's restoration, Hosea compares God's voice to that of a lion. Responding to that roar, the Jewish exiles flock home from Egypt and Assyria, trembling like frightened birds before the king of beasts (Hosea 11:10, 11). Using the same imagery, Joel prophesies the return and restoration of the Jews, with a message of judgment against the enemies of God's people (Joel 3:16). The roar of the mighty angel, then, may signal the imminence of doom against the wicked as the divine order goes forth to release God's people in the end. The fact that the vision of the mighty angel appears between the sixth and seventh trumpets may indicate that the message of doom and deliverance to the wicked and the righteous respectively takes place near the close of time.

2. Seven thunders rumble after the call of the mighty angel. It is not uncommon to find the device of thunder in the book of Revelation in the context of a revelatory episode. During the vision of God's throne room John hears peals of thunder reverberating from the throne (Rev. 4:5). Thunder booms and lightning flashes when the angel hurls fire from the golden altar to the

earth (Rev. 8:5). When God's temple in heaven opens, revealing
the ark of the covenant, heaven again fills with the sound of
thunder (Rev. 11:19). And when the seventh angel pours his bowl
of divine wrath into the air, John hears a loud voice from the
temple announcing the end of the seven plagues of God's
judgment. It is accompanied by the crash of thunder (Rev. 16:18).
Thus, in the symbolism of the Apocalypse, thunder denotes
warning and judgment.

Apparently the seven thunders have a coherent message,
since John was about to write it down. But a voice from heaven
expressly instructs him to seal up the message of the seven
thunders and forbids him to write it down (Rev. 10:4). Such a
command seems strange, in view of the heavenly orders John
received at the beginning (Rev. 1:10, 19). It reminds us of the
mandate given to Daniel to shut up the words and seal the book
(Dan. 12:4). In Daniel's case the sealing was temporary, and
simply meant a delay in the time of disclosure, but with John it
appears to be permanent.[3]

3. The angel announces the end of the time delays.[4] The
prophet sees the mighty angel lift his right hand to heaven and
take an oath in the name of the eternal Creator. The ritual of
lifting one's hand in oath-taking is ancient, and we can trace it
back to the patriarchal period (Gen. 14:22, 23). But the imagery in
our present passage clearly derives from the book of Daniel.
There in vision the prophet observes a man clothed in linen,
standing above the waters of a stream with both hands raised to
heaven, and he hears the divine messenger swear by One who
lives for ever and ever. The vision concerns a time prophecy, and
the prophetic pronouncement comes in response to Daniel's
inquiry as to the time of the end. Before the end can take place,
there must be a "shattering of the power of the holy people"
(Dan. 12:7). Until that occurs, God's people must wait patiently.

This period—stated here as "a time, two times, and half a
time"—may be seen as a time delay. The blessing toward the end
of the chapter (verse 12), pronounced on those who patiently
await the time of the end, suggests not only that God's people
must endure tribulation but that they must have the endurance
that will enable them to persevere through the postponement or
delay of the end. It is against such a background, then, that we
should understand the announcement of the mighty angel in
John's vision. In doing so, we suggest the following conclusions:
a. The statement that there will be no more delay refers to time

prophecies. No longer will God give messages to His servants, whether they be warnings or woes, that will extend the time of sin. b. The end-time that the divine messenger refers to in the book of Daniel is the same time period that the mighty angel of Revelation 10 has in mind (see Rev. 1:3, "for the time is near"). c. The message sealed by Daniel must now be revealed to John and through John to the church. And it consists of the little scroll in the hand of the mighty angel.

4. The angel declares that the time has come to reveal the mystery of God. We note several things about his statement. a. The wording is intriguing. Usually we expect prophecies to be fulfilled and mysteries to be revealed. In this case the prophecy and mystery are bound together, so that when the mystery is disclosed the prophecy is at the same time fulfilled. The mystery of God is not abstract information about the secrets of the universe. It has to do with an event through which He will make known His redemptive purpose. b. The mystery of God is something that He announces to His servants the prophets. The text recalls the statement of Amos, "Surely the Lord God does nothing, without revealing his secret to his servants the prophets" (Amos 3:7). The prophet had in mind the coming judgment against Israel, an event that was strange indeed. Israel traditionally thought of the day of the Lord as the moment when God delivered His people from the hand of the enemy, and so people commonly called it a day of light. But now it would be a day of darkness, because in their persistent wickedness the nation had become an enemy to God's redemptive purpose. The Lord has made known the mystery of the coming judgment to Amos, so that when destruction arrives the people will know and understand why it happened. In John's vision the angel refers to God *announcing* His mystery but not *revealing* it to His servants the prophets. For John the revelation of God's mystery will occur at the end-time.

c. The mystery of God will be fulfilled when the seventh angel sounds his trumpet. The book of Daniel gives repeated emphasis to God opening His mysteries to His servant Daniel (Dan. 2:17-19, 22, 29, 30, 47; 4:9, 18; 5:11, 12). But as to the mystery of the time of the end, the Lord did not disclose that to him. Instead, the angel told him to shut up the words and seal the book for those living in the end-time. For then at that period, knowledge will increase and the wise will understand (Dan. 12:1,3, 4, 10). Once again we must keep in mind that the mystery of God has to do with the completion of His redemptive work or the fulfillment of His redemptive purpose which brings about the end of human history. What God purposed in Creation and made possible through the blood of the Lamb (Rev. 5:9, 10) will be brought to completion at that time. In that day God will break the power of evil and overthrow the rule of Satan forever. He will permanently eradicate sin and death from the universe. And the wisdom and love of God will be clearly manifested with respect to His handling of the problem of evil.

The Prophet's Experience (Rev. 10:8-11)   The voice from heaven that commanded John to seal up the message of the seven thunders speaks again to him, telling him to take the little scroll from the hand of the mighty angel. And John proceeds to obey the heavenly voice, but when he does so, the mighty angel further instructs him to eat the scroll. When John obeys he discovers that it is sweet as honey in his mouth but bitter in his stomach, as the angel had said it would be (see Eze. 3:1-3). As we noted earlier, John's experience closely parallels that of the prophet Ezekiel. But several other passages also shed light on the significance of this symbolic act. The prophet Jeremiah wrote, "Thy words were found, and I ate them, and thy words became to me a joy and the delight of my heart" (Jer. 15:16). Concerning God's word, the psalmist exclaimed, "How sweet are thy words to my taste, sweeter than honey to my mouth!" (Ps. 119:103).

John's eating the little scroll in the visionary experience signifies his complete assimilation of the message that God had commissioned him to preach. Before he can communicate God's word to the nations, he has to internalize the revelation so that the divine word will become human flesh. He will then be able to proclaim the message with understanding and conviction. As with Ezekiel, so with John, the eating of the scroll is linked to his commission to preach, a fact that provides a clue as to the contents of the scroll. It has to do with the experience of the church.

The sweet-bitter effect of the scroll on the seer suggests the vicissitudes endured by God's people in the last days. We have already seen the close similarities between Revelation 10 and Daniel 12. The declaration of the mighty angel that there will be no more delay is to be understood, then, against the background of the angel's instruction to Daniel to seal up the words of the prophecy until the time of the end. The time has come now for Daniel's message to be revealed. It is therefore in its unveiling and in making its contents known that the seer experiences the sweet-bitter sensation.

Daniel 12 begins with a reference to the "time of trouble," a period "such as never has been since there was a nation" (verse 1). The text points to the great tribulation that God's people must endure before they witness the establishment of Christ's kingdom in glory. Heaven assures Daniel that his people, those whose names are "found written in the book," will be delivered. At that time there will be a resurrection of the dead, some of whom will receive everlasting life, while others will be sentenced to everlasting shame and contempt (Dan. 12:1, 2).

Some have understood the sweet-bitter experience of the faithful in the setting of the time of trouble. The joy that comes to the saints as they anticipate and prepare for the second advent of Jesus corresponds to the sweet taste of the scroll in the mouth of John, whereas the bitter sensation in the stomach of the seer represents the sorrow God's people experience as they endure persecution. Seventh-day Adventists have explained this sweet-bitter occurrence by pointing to the great disappointment of the American adventists in 1844. Because of their understanding of the prophecies of Daniel, the early adventists under the leadership of William Miller, a lay Baptist preacher, concluded that the return of Christ would take place in the fall of 1844. The expectation heightened as the believers shared the good news and made preparation for the end-time. When the date passed and the event for which they lived and labored did not take place, the adventists underwent a bitter disappointment. As a result of that disappointment many left the movement, never to return, but others saw their experience as a test of their faith and patiently accepted the ridicule and scorn handed them by unbelievers.

After John endures the sweet-bitter effect of the scroll's contents, heaven commands him to prophesy again. The wording of the text indicates the compelling aspect of the seer's commission. He has no option, but simply *must* prophesy again "about many peoples and nations and tongues and kings." He is to be obedient to the prophetic task despite the way he feels from eating the contents of the scroll. His own experience thus typifies the experience of the church during the last days. In the midst of the lingering sweet-bitter sensation, the church must fulfill the divine commission to take the gospel to the world, a world that is hostile to God's redemptive purpose. In this respect we may speak of the period as a testing occasion for the church. It is a time when God's people will face hardship and will have to suffer much in order to advance the message entrusted to them. And for those who endure the hard times God assures a place in His kingdom.

[1] *The SDA Bible Commentary,* Ellen G. White Comments, vol. 7, pp. 797, 971.

[2] Barclay, *The Revelation of John,* vol. 2, p. 54; Mounce, in *The Book of Revelation,* p. 207.

[3] Seventh-day Adventists believe that the message of the seven thunders consists of a portrayal of events occurring in connection with the proclamation of the first and second angels' messages in Revelation 14:6-8 (see *The SDA Bible Commentary,* vol. 7, pp. 797, 798).

[4] Seventh-day Adventists understand this to mean the end of prophetic time (see *The SDA Bible Commentary,* Ellen G. White Comments, vol. 7, p. 971).

Christ's Kingdom Established

(Based on Revelation 11)

"Why do the nations conspire, and the peoples plot in vain? . . . I have set my king on Zion, my holy hill" (Ps. 2:1-6).

An Overview   Revelation 11 concludes the first half of the Apocalypse. Many commentators consider the chapter to be the most difficult and the most important part of the entire book of Revelation. [1] In some respects we may see the material in chapter 11 as a summary of the essential points covered in the second half of the Apocalypse. For here we find outlined the witness of God's people in the midst of the most intense persecution. The seer introduces us to the great war between the beast and the saints, and takes us through the tragedy of tribulation to the triumph of Christ's kingdom. In capsule form we observe God's people pass from shame to glory as they withstand the ridicule and humiliation of the wicked and witness the consummation of all things in the establishment of Christ's eternal kingdom.

The Measuring of God's Temple (Rev. 11:1, 2)   In the previous chapter we observed John move from passive spectator to active participant in the vision given to him. His involvement continues in Revelation 11. Heaven gives him a measuring instrument and tells him to measure three things: the temple of God, the altar, and those who worship there. The act of measuring is symbolic, and the language and imagery derive from the book of Zechariah.

While in vision the Old Testament prophet sees a man with a measuring line in his hand, whereupon the prophet asks, "Where are you going?" The man explains that he intends to measure the city of Jerusalem. But an angel appears to the man with the measuring line and tells him that measuring the city is not necessary, for the city will be inhabited without walls, owing to the multitude of people and cattle. Moreover, the Lord Himself will be "a wall of fire," and His holy presence in their midst will provide the protection they need (Zech. 2:1-5). The prophecy of

Zechariah associates the symbolic act of measuring the city with the idea of rebuilding its walls so as to assure the residents of protection. We must keep in mind that in ancient times the only security that a city had in addition to its military forces was its surrounding wall. A wall would make it difficult for the enemy to penetrate the city and plunder its resources.

For John, then, the idea of measuring has to do with the need to rebuild and protect. That being the case, we must not understand such a need in a literal sense. Thus the prophet does not have in mind the actual reconstruction of the Jerusalem Temple, which, when he wrote, lay in ruins. And he certainly is not thinking of rebuilding the temple of God in heaven. Instead we should look elsewhere to grasp the meaning of the symbolism employed here. One suggestion is to regard the temple, the altar, and the worshipers as representing the church in its life and witness. Viewing it this way, we may interpret the act of measuring the church as God's way of preparing His people for the struggles they must face during the closing phase of the conflict with the evil powers. And it would consist of a rebuilding and a protecting. Such a work enables the church to conduct its life and ministry in a manner that fulfills the divine commission. Only in this way it will be able to ride out the storm of controversy with the forces of evil and be assured of its entrance into the heavenly kingdom. In other words, to be victorious, the church must have a clear understanding of its message, mission, and ministry. That is, it must have a saving knowledge of the truth, a grasp of mission arising from this knowledge, and an active ministry that takes its direction from this mission.

Heaven expressly orders John not to measure the court outside the temple because it is given over to the nations. The nations are forces hostile to God's redemptive purpose and are said to trample over the holy city for a period of 42 months, or 1,260 days (Rev. 11:2, 3). We may understand such symbolism more clearly when we see it against the background of New Testament times. The Temple of Herod had two courts, an inner one and an outer one. The inner court contained three sections: the court of the women, the court of Israel, and the court of the priests. The outer court was called the Court of the Gentiles, and a physical barrier separated it from the inner one. It is the outer court that John refers to in the figurative language of his vision. The nations, or the Gentiles, do not belong to the community of believers. The symbolic act of giving the outer court over to the

Gentiles involves their trampling over the holy city.

Once again we note language and imagery drawn from the book of Daniel. In a vision the Old Testament prophet saw a ghastly beast appear on the scene to make war against the saints. The creature uttered words of blasphemy against the Most High and wore out the saints by its vicious trampling (Dan. 7:7, 8, 25) for a designated period of time. [2] His blasphemy and trampling involved casting down the truth and committing sacrilege against the temple (Dan. 8:9-14).

The Holy City, then, is a reference to the people of God who have suffered persecution and have witnessed the efforts of the evil forces to corrupt and destroy God's truth, particularly as it relates to the heavenly sanctuary, or temple, and its services. It is this truth that God, through His people, must restore, and in the process He prepares His people for the end-time.

The Two Witnesses (Rev. 11:3-6) The voice that commanded John to measure the temple, the altar, and the worshipers continues. Scripture does not identify it, but we may believe that it comes from heaven and speaks with great authority. John hears it mention two witnesses who will receive power to prophesy during the period designated for the nations to trample over the people of God, that is a period of 42 months, or 1,260 days. That it involves a time of intense persecution and bitter sorrow we find indicated by the clothing worn by the witnesses. They prophesy while dressed in sackcloth.

Commentators offer a variety of suggestions as to their identity. John provides the following clues: 1. They are "the two olive trees and the two lampstands which appear before the Lord of the earth" (Rev. 11:4). The description reminds one of Zechariah's vision of the lampstand and the olive trees. In it the prophet sees two branches from two olive trees beside two golden pipes from which the oil pours out for the lamps in the sanctuary. The olive branches that supply the oil are said to be the "two anointed who stand by the Lord of the whole earth" (Zec. 4:12-14). While the passage is an obvious source for John, we note the freedom that is so typical of his use of Scripture. The prophecy of Zechariah has one lampstand, whereas John has two, and he treats the two olive trees and the two lampstands as representing the same thing, namely the two witnesses.

2. Supernatural powers protect the witnesses during the period of their prophetic activity. The same force that enables them to prophesy provides them with the ability to defend

themselves. Fire breaks forth from their mouths and consumes those who attempt to harm them. The imagery recalls the time when Elijah called fire down from heaven and destroyed his enemies (2 Kings 1:10, 12). John uses the imagery to portray the potency of the prophetic word.

3. They have power to cause droughts. Again we have another allusion to the prophetic ministry of Elijah, specifically his announcement of a drought that lasted for three and one-half years (1 Kings 17:1). The prophet began his ministry at a time of deep spiritual crisis. Ahab was king in Israel and had married Jezebel, a Phoenician princess who managed to support the worship of Baal by means of the royal treasury. According to pagan belief, Baal, the Canaanite storm god, assured the farmers a successful crop by sending rain at the right season. Elijah's action thus struck at the very heart of Baal worship.

4. They have power to change water into blood. Now John shifts attention from Elijah to Moses. Here we note a reference to the first plague of Egypt (Ex. 7:14-24). Moses initiated it at God's instruction because Pharaoh refused to release Israel.

5. They can "smite the earth with any plague, as often as they desire" (Rev. 11:6). Once again John alludes to the experience of Moses in Egypt. Despite Pharaoh's resistance to the expressed command of God, Moses was able to persist and prevail. Eventually the country of Egypt lay desolate, its vaunted military forces destroyed, while God's people were free. The latter journeyed out of Egypt under the leadership of Moses and the lordship of the Almighty One (Ex. 14:30, 31).

The activity of the two witnesses resembles the roles of Moses and Elijah. But it would be a mistake to conclude that John had them in mind. In any case, we find no compelling reason to interpret the symbolism in a strictly literal way. It makes better sense to explain the references in a figurative manner.

During New Testament times it was common to hear Jews speak of Elijah (Matt. 16:14; 17:10-12; 27:47, 49), since tradition regarded him as the forerunner of the Messiah (Mal. 4:5, 6). In time the Jews employed the name Elijah as a reference to the prophets as a whole. A similar development took place in respect to the name Moses. It became a synonym for the law (Luke 16:31; 24:27; John 7:19, 22, 23; 9:28, 29). Moses and Elijah would thus represent the law and the prophets, or together constitute the Scriptures. On the Mount of Transfiguration they appeared with

Jesus in glory, indicating that Jesus is glorified in the law and prophets, for they bear witness to the truth concerning Him (Matt. 17:3). But the two represent the witness of the Old Testament. In the New Testament we have eyewitnesses to the words and deeds of Jesus, and to His saving death and resurrection. Apart from their testimony the witness to the truth of God in Christ would indeed be incomplete.

It seems best, therefore, to understand the two witnesses in Revelation 11 as the Word of God as it finds expression through the preaching and teaching offices of the body of believers. That is to say, the church, insofar as it conducts its life and witness under the lordship of Christ and guidance of the Holy Spirit, can provide a faithful testimony to the truth. The oil from the olive branch enables the lamp to give light, and the oil represents the ministry of the Holy Spirit. Apart from the Spirit of God, the church can provide no witness, for it has no light.

The Beast and the Two Witnesses (Rev. 11:7-10)   When the two witnesses fulfill their prophetic ministry, heaven removes the divine protection afforded them, and they become vulnerable to the malicious assaults of the enemy. At this time John sees in vision the beast arising from the bottomless pit. It determines to wage war against the two witnesses. John has already introduced us to the bottomless pit in connection with the trumpet blast of the fifth angel (Rev. 9:1). With the opening of the shaft of the pit, smoke arose, and after the smoke, demonic locusts sprang forth to inflict their terrors upon the wicked inhabitants of the earth. Now John tells us that the beast ascends from the same pit to perform his evil. It is our first introduction to the beast, but the definite article suggests that John has already established its identity. From John's description of the beast's activity we note the following facts:

1. The beast draws its power and takes its direction from the demonic world, a point clear from the fact that it ascends from the bottomless pit, the haunt of demons. 2. The beast is hostile to God's saving purpose. When it rises from the pit, it singles out the two witnesses for attack, and it emerges victoriously from the conflict. 3. The beast publicly disgraces the bodies of the slain witnesses by allowing them to remain in the street of the great city for several days. To the Jewish mind, it was an act bordering on sacrilege to leave a corpse unattended and unburied. The Old Testament lists it as one of the great evils committed by the pagans against God's people (Ps. 79:1-4). Such gross inhumanity

is a mark of the demonic, and when humans commit such acts, it points to the depth of their degradation. 4. The beast conducts the war and commits the indignities in the great city, which John refers to allegorically as Sodom and Egypt. The Old Testament depicts Sodom as an extremely wicked city. Its depravity became so horrible in God's sight that He found it necessary to destroy it completely. Among the most heinous offenses were the debased acts of immorality that had become commonplace (Gen. 19:1-11). Egypt is not a city but a nation. Whereas Sodom represented the depths of immorality, Egypt typified oppression and slavery.

The beast's followers exemplify its own base character. For the three and one half days that the slain witnesses remain in the street of the great city, men from the peoples, tribes, tongues, and nations come to gaze and gawk over their dead bodies. It is a time for the wicked to celebrate the beast's victory. Their festivity resembles that of a holiday. They rejoice, make merry, and exchange presents. But there is something extremely wrong about their celebration. It is morbid despite their fiendish delight. They refuse to allow anyone to bury the bodies of the slain witnesses, so that they may rejoice with hellish glee over their pale corpses (Rev. 11:9, 10).

The Resurrection and Ascension of the Witnesses (Rev. 11:11-13)   The pagan world's merrymaking is brief. A breath of life from God enters the bodies of the two witnesses, and immediately they stand up on their feet. A great fear falls over the followers of the beast who see the resurrection. The picture recalls on a much smaller scale Ezekiel's vision of the valley of the dry bones. There God had instructed him to prophesy to the dry bones and to the breath that was to enter the dry bones, and upon doing so, the breath entered those who were slain, and they came alive and stood on their feet (Eze. 37:1-10).

After the resurrection of the two witnesses John hears a loud voice from heaven, which summons them. Then in the sight of their enemies they ascend to heaven in a cloud. The scene alludes to the ascension of Elijah in a chariot of fire and a whirlwind (2 Kings 2:11, 12). And at that time a great earthquake occurs that devastates one tenth of the city and kills 7,000 of its inhabitants. The impact of the earthquake on the survivors is similar to the effect produced by the resurrection of the witnesses: it terrifies them so that in a state of terror they give glory to God.

It is not clear as to whether the wicked genuinely repent in the face of such wonders or simply find themselves compelled to acknowledge the almighty sovereignty of God. In view of their repugnant perversity (Rev. 11:9, 10), it seems unlikely that they would be capable of genuine repentance. Whatever the case, their acknowledgment of God's preeminence constitutes an appropriate vindication of the two witnesses and a proper prelude to the trumpet blast of the seventh angel.

Seventh-day Adventists have believed that the material in Revelation 11 accurately depicts in a symbolic way the conditions in France during the period of the First French Republic (1792-1804). It was a time when antireligious bias swept across the nation, resulting in a decree in Paris that abolished religion. Adventists have thus seen the assault of the beast against the two witnesses as a symbolic portrayal of the attack by French ruling powers against the Holy Scriptures. The resurrection and exaltation of the two witnesses would then find fulfillment in the establishment of national Bible societies, the most important of which were the British and Foreign Bible Society, founded in 1804, and the American Bible Society, organized in 1816. [3]

The Word of God has survived the demonic assaults of peoples, nations, and pagan belief systems throughout the centuries. The human pawns of Satan have come and gone, but the Word of God remains sovereign in the hearts and lives of His people. The time will soon come when the forces of evil in full demonic strength will organize an offensive against God's Word and His church, but they will fail and will at last be obliterated from God's universe.

The Seventh Trumpet: The Consummation of History (Rev. 11:14-19)   Immediately preceding the seventh trumpet blast, John announces that the second woe has passed, and the third is soon to come. Commentators differ as to what constitutes the third woe. We find one clue in the announcement from heaven following the overthrow of Satan and his evil cohorts: "Rejoice then, O heaven and you that dwell therein! But woe to you, O earth and sea, for the devil has come down to you in great wrath, because he knows that his time is short!" (Rev. 12:12).

Following the sounding of the seventh angel's trumpet, John hears loud voices in heaven, saying, "The kingdom of the world has become the kingdom of our Lord and of his Christ, and he shall reign for ever and ever" (Rev. 11:15). Here is the most thrilling message in the book of Revelation, the good news that God's people in every age and in every nation have yearned to hear. It fulfills the Messianic expectations of the prophets, answers the patient inquiries of the oppressed, and satisfies the pleas of the martyrs. The angelic hosts themselves announce this declaration of triumph, and it consists of two parts: 1. It proclaims the transfer of dominion and rule of our world to God and His Christ. The wording reflects the language of Psalm 2:2, a Messianic psalm, which the early Christian community applied to Jesus. The decree indicates that God will share His rule with Christ. 2. Their rule is eternal. The use of the singular pronoun ("he shall reign") adds emphasis to the unity that exists between God and Christ Jesus.

A hymn of thanksgiving from the 24 elders follows the declaration of the angelic hosts. The hymn centers attention on God's manifestation of His great power in the final conflict as He overthrows the evil forces and begins His reign. Once again we note a reference to Psalm 2, which speaks of the nations conspiring and of the people plotting against the Lord and His Anointed. But God's wrath brought the raging nations to their knees in defeat (Rev. 11:18). The triumph of God's wrath is a recurring theme in the second half of the book (Rev. 14:10, 11; 16:15-21; 20:8, 9).

In their hymn of thanksgiving, the elders identify three great events that follow the defeat of the evil powers and the establishment of God's rule: 1. The work of judgment. The time has come for the dead to be judged. What Scripture means here is the judgment of the wicked. God will give His judicial decision and execute the verdict at the end of the thousand-year period (Rev. 20:11-15).

2. The matter of rewarding God's servants, the prophets, the saints, and everyone, small and great who fears His name. Their reward appears in the vision of the New Jerusalem descending from heaven to the new earth, where God Himself will dwell (Rev. 21:1-4).

3. The final act in the great drama of redemption. It consists of the complete eradication of sin and death, of Satan and his evil hosts, from the universe (Rev. 20:7-10).

The vision ends with a scene of God's temple and the ark of the covenant within the temple. It is a view of the Most Holy Place, from which proceed the promise of God's protection during the last days, and the threat of His impending wrath. From God's throne the saints receive assurances of deliverance and the wicked can expect judgment. What follows the opening of the temple is the recurring phenomena of flashes of lightning, voices, and peals of thunder. In addition, we note the reference to an earthquake and heavy hail. The first half of the book, ends on a note that one might interpret either ominously or joyously. The choice is ours to make.

"The Spirit and the Bride say, 'Come.' And let him who hears say, 'Come.' And let him who is thirsty come, let him who desires take the water of life without price" (Rev. 22:17).

[1] Barclay, *The Revelation of John*, vol. 2, p. 65.
[2] *The SDA Bible Commentary*, vol. 7, p. 801.
[3] *Ibid.*, pp. 802, 803.